How to Find Peacefulness

Tina Jefferies

I dedicate this book to my husband and sons, who have lived respectfully and acceptingly as I have made my journeys into solitude.

Tina Jefferies has worked with people throughout her 30-year career as a lecturer, coach, counsellor, and leadership and management consultant, and has discovered that that, however successful, motivated, willing or able individuals are, knowingly or unknowingly they are in search of elusive peacefulness. Through leading retreats, and coaching and counselling people to establish patterns of time-alone experiences within hectic lifestyles, she has helped many learn the skills to discover peacefulness for themselves within their hard-pressed lives.

Teach Yourself®

How to Find Peacefulness

Tina Jefferies

The publisher has used its best endeavours to ensure that any website addresses referred to in this book are correct and active at the time of going to press. However, the publisher and the author have no responsibility for the websites and can make no guarantee that a site will remain live or that the content will remain relevant, decent or appropriate.

The publisher has made every effort to mark as such all words which it believes to be trademarks. The publisher should also like to make it clear that the presence of a word in the book, whether marked or unmarked, in no way affects its legal status as a trademark.

Every reasonable effort has been made by the publisher to trace the copyright holders of material in this book. Any errors or omissions should be notified in writing to the publisher, who will endeavour to rectify the situation for any reprints and future editions.

Cover image © Oleksandr Rozhkov – Fotolia

Typeset by Cenveo® Publisher Services.

Printed in Great Britain by CPI Group (UK) Ltd, Croydon, CR0 4YY.

Hodder & Stoughton policy is to use papers that are natural, renewable and recyclable products and made from wood grown in sustainable forests. The logging and manufacturing processes are expected to conform to the environmental regulations of the country of origin.

Hodder & Stoughton Ltd

338 Euston Road

London NW1 3BH

www.hodder.co.uk

Also available in ebook

Acknowledgements

Many experiences have influenced me in the writing of this book, from escapes to country cottages to peaceful moments at mountain-top vistas, for which I am thankful. But, most particularly, I am grateful to the many and varied *people* who have inspired my life journey. Some I know well; others simply have made cameo appearances. However, most especially, I would like to acknowledge my life partner, friend and husband, Nick, for honourably supporting the twists and turns of my explorations. Grateful thanks also go to Robert Anderson, for his sympathetic editing, and the team at Hodder for making the book a reality.

Contents

Preface

Today we rarely hear the word 'peacefulness' outside the context of religious, quasi-religious or spiritual experience – except, perhaps, in brochures inviting us to enjoy a pampering session at a spa or a weekend away in a country hotel. Nonetheless, in today's hectic, technology-driven world the promise of peacefulness remains an attractive one – hence all those spas and country hotels – though, sadly, it is one that is only rarely fulfilled. For most of us, 'peacefulness' means snatching a five-minute break in between finishing work and picking up the kids, or on a train journey between business meetings. It remains a kind of utopian ideal, something surely impossible to realize with today's accelerating lifestyles.

In this book, I want to show how real peacefulness *is* obtainable, but also that it is something that has to be created, practised and worked at, something that has to be deliberately integrated into the texture of our lives. Learning peacefulness is above all a practical journey. It is not found in quick fixes, fancy fads or mystic mantras, but in a thoughtful and ongoing balancing of our energy and time, of engagement and solitude. Finding peacefulness demands commitment, discipline, and, yes, hard work, but it can be a satisfying and enlightening journey, one that can alleviate stress and redirect our steps towards different kinds of success.

Peacefulness is about much more than just release from busyness. It has its own positive value. It helps us to appreciate time spent with ourselves; it enables us to reflect on the things that truly matter to us and to discover new perspectives on our lives. Increasing numbers of people talk of peacefulness as thoughtfulness and mindfulness, as an awareness of the moment, as an immersive engagement with the here and now. Above all, though, I want to show how finding peacefulness can be liberating.

My hope is that this book will encourage you to find the beauty in peacefulness and that it will form a gateway to your own personal journey.

Tina Jefferies

November 2012

1

Why am I So Busy?

In this chapter you will learn:

▶ *about some of the factors that cause busyness*

▶ *about how to recognize the signs of over-commitment*

▶ *about how to begin a journey towards peacefulness.*

How do you feel?

Before you read this chapter, ask yourself the following self-assessment questions:

1 What predominantly fills up your time?

2 What proportion of your time is filled by work, family, and socializing?

3 How often do you feel the pressure to respond to instantaneous demands and communications?

4 Are you easily distracted?

5 How much time do you spend alone?

A countercultural message

There are so few empty pages in my engagement pad, or empty hours in the day, or empty rooms in my life in which to stand alone and find myself. Too many activities, and people, and things. Too many worthy activities, valuable things, and interesting people. For it is not merely the trivial which clutters our lives but the important as well. We can have a surfeit of treasures...

Anne Morrow Lindbergh, *Gift from the Sea*

In today's world teaching yourself peacefulness might seem almost a countercultural concept. So many self-help books encourage you to be more motivated, more successful, better, richer... Their power-driven titles raise expectations: life-transforming changes are promised in return for very little effort, offering quick-fire ways to manage your time more efficiently, make better decisions and so on. But after the initial bout of inspiration, how much of these messages do we really take in, let alone implement?

The message of this book is altogether different. If you learn just one lasting lesson from this book, it should simply be to welcome more solitude and peacefulness into your life. In this book I want you to find your *own* pathway, to journey at your *own* pace, to listen to your *own* body and your *own* inner being with a deeper respect and understanding for the unique person you are, and the contribution you make to the world.

Learning peacefulness is like investing in a longer-term savings plan. By practising some of the ideas that you will discover in this book, you will build a resource that will grow over time, but with the added bonus that you will be able to draw on it while saving it! Moreover, what you learn about yourself in the peacefulness of solitude will be an invaluable lifelong investment. Putting aside an amount of time every day before you set yourself to any pursuit, whether work, family or social, will focus you, centre you and teach you.

Key idea: The secret power of peacefulness

Peacefulness sounds, at first glance, like a passive, effortless state. However, as soon as we are able to look past blind ambition, and are not caught up in the constant pursuit of progress, we are able to invite wisdom in, and see the hidden power of peacefulness – something that has the power to transform our lives in ways undreamed of by self-help books or personal development manuals. It's a pearl of great price awaiting discovery.

Where does it all begin?

As babies, we learn to crawl, walk and then run. As young adults, it is easy to believe that we need to *keep* running in order to keep pace with, or even be ahead of, the crowd. Education accentuates the phenomenon, especially in the past 20 to 25 years where the focus has been fixed firmly on the attainment of examination grades, with little regard for the other avenues of personal achievement and enrichment.

This formative time is when the pace is set, and it's a pace that only gathers momentum as life presents more and more opportunities and challenges for us to seize and face up to. Obstacles are simply hurdles to leap with gusto; it's easy, *if* you run at them with sufficient speed and skill to jump clear every time.

We now think that a good life balance consists of managing to drive ourselves through several gym sessions a week, maintaining a healthy diet, and being in constant, multi-platform communication with friends and acquaintances, on top, of course, of coping with long hours at work. But this isn't balance, but a juggling act. One where the ball frequently gets dropped – in the form of our health and wellbeing, and the quality of our relationships.

So all this busyness can be self-defeating. Legs tire, energies dwindle, spirits sag, especially when pathways are not clear and the pace too driven. The more we try to leap, the hurdles become higher, the race tougher, and sometimes less enjoyable. Burn-out is endemic to modern living, so it's no surprise that so many people at least dream about downsizing, about escaping to the country with the family, in pursuit of a simpler, quieter and gentler life. Life – such people have realized – is not a race but a *journey*. A journey that we need to respect.

This learning to walk, even crawl again, provides a new and refreshing perspective, a quality life that's worth living. We begin to look at life once again through the fresh, wide eyes of the child, and busyness makes way for new sights, sounds and experiences.

 Remember this: An old saying…

There is an old saying: 'If the devil can't make you bad, he'll make you busy.' That's certainly something to think about in our stuffed-to-capacity lives!

The fear of silence

Amid our full-on lives we sometimes catch ourselves yearning for peace and quiet. We long for a space in your life now and again. Just a pause for breath, please! But as soon we get that peace and quiet we begin to feel uncomfortable, even afraid. Ask yourself: Do you really like the idea of being alone? Or do you secretly fear the silence? And when a moment of quiet does finally arrive, does it fail to give you the reward you yearned for? Does your mind just turn over and over and peacefulness remain as elusive as a butterfly?

The solution is making peacefulness a *part* of your life, not simply an added luxury.

Case study

'I hated being alone. When faced with just myself, I was afraid that I might not like what I found! I preferred to have people around me, yet knew that sometimes I found it hard to think clearly and get my own perspective on things. I just didn't know how to be alone. But, after I began to spend a few minutes every morning on my own, before the family got up, I started to enjoy this alone time and to appreciate that it fulfilled a need I didn't know I had. It also helped to ground my day.'

A switching off from all contact can be eerie. Silence feels deafening. So, we fill a quiet moment with some kind of distraction instead. Television, radio, computers and phones are frequently resorted to as ways of filling the void. Rather than remaining in the quiet we fill it obsessively. Being stimulated by noise and engagement seems a necessity, proving we are not alone, and validating our existence by engaging us with the world beyond ourselves. It also provides evidence that we are not 'wasting' time by merely drifting along.

Key idea: Silence really is golden

So much is learned in silence. It provides a chance to gain a little distance and perspective at the front line of living, a source of energy and power. Try it rather than buy it. Silent reflection costs nothing, but it is worth gold.

So, typically, 'refreshment' and 'recuperation' comes in the form of a trip to the bar with friends, a lavish session at the beauty parlour or spa, retail therapy or as many trips to the golf course as can be squeezed in between everything else. We are consuming our way through life, gorging on as many experiences as possible, at as fast a pace as we can keep up.

Is this *really* fulfilling our human needs and satisfying the desires and longings of our souls? Are these experiences turning us into integrated and wise individuals? Probably not, we would be the first to admit, though there isn't time to think about it! The slower-paced lifestyle appears as a mere waste of time and opportunity. Surely our lives are dull and not worth while if there are too many moments empty of specific, measurable activity.

The classic advice found in many self-help books – something adopted from management spheres – is summed up in the acronym SMART, meaning Specific, Measurable, Realistic Targets, and is being applied to almost every area of life. You've got to, it says, be specific about your goals, weigh up their worth, make sure they're realistic, and, above all, *achieve* them! All this becomes an insidious driving force in our lives, leaving little room for unscripted, unscheduled reflection. Yet it is from reflection that emerges the truly creative, energized and rewarding life.

The superabundance of 'experience' and the richness of solitude

The hunger for every kind of experience is the condition and aspiration of modern human beings. Time in solitude is considered a dispensable activity when compared to the many ways you can entertain yourself. Many live as if they have to cram in as much as possible during their short time spent on Earth. Ironically, however, the faster we live, the shorter our lives feel. Knowing that we cannot do it *all* might actually be quite liberating, extending our sense of the *duration* of our lives.

What is at risk, amid the bombardment of distractions and demands on our time, is the ability to think clearly for ourselves. When we are perpetually preoccupied and constantly stimulated by distractions, we lose time itself – and that quiet, still place where we can learn most about who we are and what is of real and lasting value in our lives. This is the place where you begin to stop making the superficial decisions, and start to think more slowly and deeply and reflect on what truly matters.

Solitude is a place where you learn much that is of value about yourself. In the company of others, it is easier to reveal only little pieces of the person you are, or want to be seen as. Being alone creates a place for honest personal reflection. It provides you with a truthful account of your needs, hopes and fears, and a map showing you the way towards wisdom and a greater understanding of not only yourself but of others, too.

Remember this: A life without solitude...

Without periods of solitude, your personal needs, desires and character traits remain unexamined. They continue to exist and are lost among the competing crowd of externally driven thoughts, demands and expectations. Personal growth is inhibited.

If you find you are wearied by constant involvement and information processing, in danger of burn-out owing to over-activity, you may find that some regular time alone, just for a few minutes each day or each week, is of great benefit to you. But how do you change what appears to be an inherent part of modern living?

Case study

'It wasn't until I began scheduling one day a month in my diary to myself that I was able to let go of some of the things I thought I should be doing, but found I didn't really need to. It gave me the opportunity to have no demands placed on me for just one day. I became a better person just for that because I gained a fresh perspective on my life that helped me both at home and at work.'

It is worth remembering that you do have choice. Free choice is a wonderful thing, but you have to have the appropriate awareness before making choices. As I was writing the passage above, my mobile phone bleeped, indicating that I had received a text message. The instant reaction to an instant message would have been to check it. I chose my response: leave it and read later. One small decision to defer an instant reaction and respond at another, *chosen* time brings me back in control over that phone in my pocket. Back in control of the way I choose to live life.

A note in music gains significance from the silences on either side.

Anne Morrow Lindbergh, *Gift from the Sea*

Try it now: Take a moment...

Take a pause now and recall/recount: *How many times in your day do you feel you have to react spontaneously to an instant message or demand?*

The point is that so often we *react* rather than make *considered responses*. This is at the driving seat of motivation when we are faced with electronic communications. The habit frequently extends, however, to relationships and other activities, too. Expectations are created that we are all available 24/7.

You do have a choice! Slow down, think, don't just react, and stop being permanently available.

Distractions and reactions

What are the specific distractions in our modern lives? Distractions can be attributed to lifestyle, emotions or simply visual stimuli. They might come by way of pressure to possess certain things and do certain activities (lifestyle), be caused by our concerns about or feelings of responsibility for ourselves, others and their situations (emotional), or entertainments and environmental messages that attract or demand our attention (visual). Let's look at each of these in turn:

▶ *Lifestyle* The choices you make about what you want to do or have, and why you do it or have it, should be based upon your *own* ideas and expectations. However, when bombarded by a myriad of options and opinions, these choices are also influenced by factors such as popular opinion, trends and so on. Getting to know yourself far better during times of complete solitude helps you become clearer about what is truly of value and what is not. You cut through the highly seductive external distractions and learn what suits you best.

▶ *Emotional* These distractions draw you into the feelings you have about certain people or circumstances as well as into your own. Overthinking, worry, and fear are some of the more negative aspects of these distractions and can be linked to exaggerated expectations of happiness.

▶ *Visual* These distractions draw you into noticing and reading the environmental messages that surround us. When you walk into a room where there's a television or a computer on in the corner, your eyes will always be drawn to it. We are easily hooked by visual and emotional priming, particularly through advertising and other media messages.

Of course, these distractions are often interlinked. For example, *visual* distractions such as television, the Internet, magazines, newspapers, and advertising hoardings send us subliminal and seductive messages that stimulate ideas about what constitutes a fulfilling *lifestyle,* and engage our *emotions* – our needs and insecurities – at a deep and insidious level.

Remember this: Perpetual motion

The brain is in an almost constant state of alert, to the point that it becomes weary and numbed trying to handle the volume of information and perpetual stimulus thrown at it. In our modern, media-saturated world we therefore risk operating in fazed, dummy-like mode most of the time.

Walk down the average shopping street and you will notice the huge volume (in both senses!) of 'environmental' messages designed to get your attention. Both consciously and unconsciously you will be processing a vast array of messages at any one time. In the current economic climate, businesses are scrabbling even harder to grab your attention, and whether it's a hoarding or a cluster of well-placed tables and chairs, luring you to sit awhile with a cup of coffee, so much is designed to steer your decisions in the direction that others want you to go. And all the time you are moving away from the true you and are being denied true peacefulness.

Key idea: Shed those distractions

Begin to shed the unnecessary distractions by raising your awareness of the many things in your average day that disrupt your concentration and, let's face it, eat away at your time. Begin to bring your attention back into the moment. Don't answer your ringing mobile phone at the cash desk in the supermarket. Give the person who is serving you your full attention. It is perfectly possible for you to let the phone call wait!

During time given to contemplation and peaceful solitude, our working memory is rested and restored. Clear thinking and other cognitive functions need this time out. 'When people aren't being bombarded by external stimuli, their brains can, in effect, relax,' writes Nicholas Carr (2012). 'They no longer have to tax their working memories by processing a stream of bottom-up distractions. The resulting state of contemplativeness strengthens their ability to control their mind.'

Doing it all

Over-commitment is common in our highly accessible world. Our choices seem almost limitless: when confronted with what to have, what to do, what to be, there has never been so much opportunity, so much choice. Hence, many people are drawn into overload. Trying to accomplish just a little bit of everything is often the solution to the dilemmas this imposes upon us.

There are children I know who go to an after-school activity every night of the school week, and who consequently have very little free-flow, free-choice time. There are retired people I know who rarely have a day free because their weeks are packed with so many clubs, societies and days out. It's crazy! Of course, going to that life class or bowling tournament is not harmful in itself (these activities can be rewarding, of course), but a relentless succession of stimulating activities not offset by periods of quiet and solitude means that a deeper *quality* of life is forfeited.

Remember this: You can't have it all!

We can't have it all and do it all without something in our lives suffering as a direct result. This might be a feeling of emptiness. *Quality* of experiences rather than *quantity* is more important.

Try it now: Recognize the signs of over-commitment

We easily become over-committed at home and work, by slowly adding extra activities. It is therefore important to review your commitments and make decisions *before* you over-commit. Keep over-commitment in check.

For example, ask yourself: Do I...

* have the time to take a day off now and again, to stop and do nothing very much?
* have the time to appraise not only *what* I am doing, but *why* I do it?
* feel my life is rushing by with barely time to take a breath?
* really value each commitment I have for its own sake?

Consider all the activities you are involved in, whether at home or work, whether it's leisure or social. By reflecting on the real value of each individual thing, begin to see just how critical it is – or not.

A small beginning

Peacefulness is achievable despite the noise and fullness of activity in a modern life. And it does not necessarily mean total withdrawal, retiring on a retreat or becoming a hermit! We all have responsibilities. We can move towards peacefulness simply by adopting a quieter heart, mind and body. Consider adopting the following 'philosophy':

▶ Being in the minute while you are in it engages your attention and raises your awareness of the forces and demands that are on you;

▶ Assuming a calm and collected approach to life, with a wider perspective, and not allowing frustrations and irritations to get under your skin, is by far the best way to engender peacefulness;

▶ Times of solitude help to teach you the value of the moment, especially when you learn different ways to focus your attention through simple reflective exercises.

If the prospect of long periods of time alone makes you uneasy, don't worry. Go carefully with yourself; there is no need for a rushed approach. Start by taking just a minute from time to time during each day to stop and breathe with your eyes closed. In that minute, become acutely aware of what surrounds you. Distance yourself from the phone, the television, other people and take a deep breath, physically and mentally. Stare into space for a moment. Notice the beauty of whatever it is you are staring at. If you're outside, it might be the shape of the clouds or the silent strength of a tree. Whatever you choose to spend time focusing upon will help you begin a longer journey towards greater self-awareness and self-fulfilment

Remember this: A little silence

Try starting and finishing your day with a little silence – you will learn from it and begin to enjoy and look forward to it.

We tend to relate silence or solitude to the life of the hermit, or monk. We perhaps view them as something deeply spiritual – the domain of only the creative, the pious or the downright wacky. However, in my opinion they are things that everyone should cultivate. Even at an everyday level they offer us creative spaces, windows into both the inner and outer worlds, into a place where wisdom is found.

Some believe that episodes of self-reflection should be avoided. That they're too risky! But by learning to listen to the self and to the resonating sounds within silence. we can discover meaning and satisfaction in life.

Key idea: Silence for all

Silence, solitariness and contemplation are not just for the monk, the hermit or anchorite, a 'cop-out' from 'real' life. They recharge and energize all of us and develop us in new and unexpected ways.

The value of reflection

Reflection in solitude has far-reaching value and benefits our personal life and even our professional life, too – for example:

▶ *Personal* – it provides greater understanding of what makes you tick, your values, beliefs, motivations and direction;

▶ *Professional* – it provides a broader perspective on your personal skills and attributes and how they can be utilized in the workplace and to what effect.

Daniel H. Pink, in *A Whole New Mind* (2010), speaks of the 'conceptual age' into which we are entering. Having lived through the agricultural, industrial and information ages over the last 150 years, we are now entering a more *creative* and *empathic* stage. The times are a changin' – technologies are radically transforming the way we behave and our psychology and brain responses with it. To enter this new age successfully, we must integrate head and heart. We are not machines and cannot expect to become simply extensions of them. We must use our unique human state to ride the waves of change.

Reflection is a great quality to develop in everything you do. It provides a rounded perspective. Stepping back and reviewing choices, commitments and opportunities is an important discipline to practise on a regular basis. Whether at a personal or professional level, it provides useful insight into how to face challenges squarely, be resilient to demands and make more holistically informed choices.

Key idea: Discipline

Developing personal strength and balance, despite the distractions and demands of modern life, requires discipline. It takes time and effort to exercise muscles that may have become flabby in the face of easy entertainment, lack of awareness and over-indulgence in unconsidered activity. It demands:

✳ careful attention
✳ thought and reflection
✳ development, *and*
✳ learning

in order to be aware of and understand the true value of time spent alone.

If you are used to quick fixes and instant solutions, you may find the process of letting go of certain demands in order to take time out a difficult exercise to master. However, living with periods of solitude as a regular part of your day or week is the way to achieving valuable and lasting personal insight, knowledge and development. It will soon lead you to respect its virtues.

Just being alone for few minutes or hours a day, a week, or more, might sound an impossibility and luxury you can ill afford until retirement. It is, however, a golden gateway to self-discovery and fulfilling your potential. It allows you to tap into hidden reserves, allowing you to gain from inner personal insight and development.

Mere experience, if it is not matched by deep concentration, does not translate into excellence.

Matthew Syed, *Bounce*

Many would say that holidays are the only time they have to slow the pace and perhaps have a little time alone. But so many of us return from a holiday ready for another. Holidays, too, are frequently stuffed with a myriad of activities and demands.

Very little is actually required to find a simple solitary space in your day or week. Just a few minutes are all it takes initially. Simple methods of slowing down your thinking and eliminating distractions, even though these moments are initially short in duration, will eventually reward you with more satisfying and more rehabilitating experiences than any holiday.

Standing back and reflecting in times of solitude will help you:

▶ become more selective with activities

▶ sharpen your decision-making

▶ develop the idea that less really is more

▶ not let life drive you along

▶ reflect upon and appraise your life–work balance.

Focus points

✳ Integrating peacefulness into a busy life isn't just a time-management exercise, but a grass-roots review of all your involvements.

✳ Consider: does this task, or commitment, actually add to, or deplete, my awareness and concentration?

✳ Solitude is a low-cost, highly accessible way of recovering from, and building capacity in the face of, a demanding lifestyle.

✳ Distractions can be minimized to benefit your personal effectiveness.

✳ Time alone may seem an impossible option at first, but you can start with just one minute!

✳ Thoughts, decisions and plans for action are distilled during times of solitude.

✳ Solitude can be a highly creative resource in your personal development.

Next step

You may have some questions at this point, such as:

* How can I make the time for peacefulness?
* How can I prepare an appropriate space?
* What can I usefully learn from the experience?
* How will I make a return to the busyness of life while retaining the benefits of greater personal understanding?

The following chapters will enable you to find answers to these questions and others, and help you confidently prepare to make your first steps towards taking regular time out for solitude.

The first nut to crack is learning why it is so hard to stop...

2

Can't Stop, or Won't Stop?

In this chapter you will learn:

- ▶ *How to deselect busyness*
- ▶ *About stress and success*
- ▶ *About getting used to silence.*

How do you feel?

Before you read this chapter, ask yourself the following self-assessment questions:

1 How much choice about your life or work situations do you think you have?

2 How difficult do you find it to make decisions?

3 Do you feel that you have to work faster to stand still?

4 How much would you like to have more time to yourself?

Under stress

Factory workers had to master a new set of skills and learn how to bend pixels instead of steel; many of today's knowledge workers will likewise have to command a new set of aptitudes. They'll need to do what workers abroad cannot do equally well for much less money – such as forging relationships rather than executing transactions, tackling novel challenges instead of solving routine problems, and synthesizing the big picture rather than analysing a single component.

Daniel H. Pink, *A Whole New Mind*

Today temptation waits at every corner with more things than ever to occupy or 'complete' our lives. Temptation is fine, but it requires discipline and self-control, if we are not to fall prey to the disasters that lie within it. Each purchase, each holiday, each activity experienced or gained is pretty innocent in itself, but like children in the most amazing sweetshop (haven't we all dreamed of a real Charlie's Chocolate Factory?), we are at risk of gorging ourselves on more than we can possibly consume, leading us towards frenetic, stressed, over-committed and burdened lives.

And if we maintain lives at this pace for a protracted period, we soon sit back fragmented and shattered, not really knowing what we want. We've eaten our fill and are now left facing the aftermath, confused, numbed and dumbfounded.

The phrases 'I'm stressed' or 'I'm too busy' are a constant refrain today and this is the case even, most unexpectedly, among those whose lives should be a little more balanced, a little simpler – the retired and the young. Stress can be fine in itself – after all, it's just the pressure any object is put under – but if that object is forced too much, or for too long, eventually stress cracks appear, and eventually it can even be destroyed.

Of course, the shape and robustness of the object will determine whether it can take a greater or lesser degree of stress. If we take the demands and complexity of our lives, self-selected or otherwise, to be the force upon us, our capacity to cope with the stress will depend on the robustness of the shape we are in. The shape we are in is dictated by what we choose, and have previously chosen, in life:

- *Choices* – about how you spend your time and energy and how you deploy the resources at your disposal, i.e. money, possessions, time and talent;

- *Demands* – personal requirements and responsibilities to yourself and your family and work or social commitments;

- *Distractions* – internally and externally driven factors, usually uninvited or unexpected, that draw your attention.

It is easy to believe that we do not have much choice about how busy we are. We lose all sense of peacefulness by charging on ahead and not heeding the warnings to get things into balance – quite often until it is too late.

When family, work and friendships take up the slack of our inability or refusal to stop, things become stretched and tension rises. Difficulties arise and we are not sure why. We think that more communication, more treats, more holidays and days out together and bonding will resolve it. But that, we discover, just adds further to the demand to be 'doing things' and ultimately just piles on more stress.

We won't stop! We just can't stop and simply *be still* for a while.

Remember this: Do less!

If life is pressured, you don't need more time. You need to do less.

Concentration versus alienation

When do you have the time to deeply and fully concentrate? Are you capable of spending time in deep concentration in order to improve at something? We are absorbed by so many things in our modern, technologically filled time. We like fast food, fast connections, fast information, fast fixes. Doing and acquiring things at speed does not free up our time, but takes up more of it – it absorbs us, if we are not careful. We like to *get* it, *have* it, *do* it now. We don't want it later after we've relaxed and considered the full implications. Gratification, we feel, should be instant!

The *fragmentation* of time that such lifestyle induces is not conducive to deep concentration. In fact, the average day is beset by demands and interruptions of many kinds, disintegrating our experience of time.

Deep concentration leads to excellence, says Matthew Syed, in his book *Bounce* (2011). But, how can we become excellent and reach a more lasting success through deep concentration when time does not afford us that luxury? The answer is: by prioritizing moments of *no distraction*. Alone, we find the space to think, feel, reflect and refuel, by focusing mind, body and soul.

The problem of modern life, however, is that we are increasingly prevented from having access to this deep concentration. Even as we are engaged in ever more tasks and activities, we are simultaneously alienated from them.

Conditions at work and home have changed radically in the last century, particularly with the introduction of labour-saving devices. We have machines, tools and gadgets galore – most of which are designed to make labour lighter and give us the freedom to spend our time in other ways, while the machines do it more quickly or efficiently. We are relieved of thinking about or engaging in certain tasks. Washing machines, microwave ovens and lawn mowers in the domestic sphere, automated machinery, calculators and computers in the workplace, all force us away from the hands-on engagement that our forebears experienced. We abdicate responsibility to a gadget or machine.

Because they were more actively engaged in their work – whether they were ploughing a field or typesetting a book – our forebears' minds and bodies were also more involved in the *cause* and *effect* of tasks and their outcomes. Things took more energy, thought and understanding to achieve. The *doing* was key and was fully integrated with skills that had been passed on through centuries of accumulated knowledge and wisdom. With our generation a gradual physical and mental alienation has crept in.

A calculator means you don't have to use the brain, or background knowledge, so much to work out a calculation. A washing machine means you don't have to use as much physical energy and muscle power to clean clothes. A television means you don't have to imaginatively create entertainment for yourself. Time-honoured skills and instinctive facilities have become less utilized, more and detached from the how and the why.

Working now on a need-to-know basis, we don't need to know so much about how something works, and why, when machines do it for us. We can do things faster but with far less understanding. The rising tide of virtual communication, too, means that face-to-face interaction can be ditched to a large extent. Innate skills of reading body language and facial expression are no longer employed in the same way.

Because machines liberate us from mundane activity, we can have more, consume more and, as a consequence, *be consumed* by more. Just consider our food – we have more to choose from in the supermarket than people living up to the middle of the last century could ever have imagined; more variety than previous generations would even have recognized. More choice means more decisions, a greater complexity of ideas, suggestions and options. The brain is employed in more decision-making and the body has less direct involvement in the activity.

No wonder we get mentally fatigued in this all-consuming fog!

Time

The time promised to us by means of all the labour-saving devices and gadgetry is filled by a proliferation of activities, and we even find we have *less* time than we had before. A world of opportunity, choice and plenty threatens to gobble up time if you do not take the time to stand back and reflect, to review, realign and balance. Within this scenario, negative stress takes a foothold. It devours all the wholesomeness of life, consuming it by piling on the pressure and tension.

When we know we have a task to do, a goal to achieve, responsibilities to meet, we feel guilty if we are not at least *trying* to keep up with things. Because we have so many tasks, activities and goals that we heap upon ourselves these days, we feel guilty if we are doing anything else except labouring away at them. Staying late at work and sacrificing every little bit of downtime to activities of every kind are propelled by feelings of guilt and the need to feel that we *are*.

Case study

A highly conscientious colleague who consistently worked at managing a department for longer hours than she was ever contracted for never got to the end of her 'to do' lists. There were always new things added, as she ticked each achievement off. The treadmill was moving nonstop. Though she enjoyed her work, always doing her very best and setting herself only the highest level of performance, she was weary and becoming very stressed. As a consequence, she could not maintain the standard she expected from herself. She was beginning to make the odd mistake, and felt guilty about having made those mistakes, even to the point of self-loathing. She never took her full leave entitlement, feeling she'd get too behind with work.

One day, at the beginning of a new year, I sat with her as she opened her fresh new diary, and said, 'It won't be long before that's full to bursting!' I suggested that before she wrote anything in it at all she should blank out one day each quarter to take time out. After she had overcome the shock of the mere possibility of such a self-indulgence, she did so, and gradually she began to realize the importance of letting go a little. She grasped the truth that, the tighter you hold on, the tougher it gets and the harder it becomes to step off that eternal treadmill.

It's a situation that simply leads to a vicious circle of over-commitment, guilt and self-recrimination. Short-circuit the process by:

▶ allowing yourself the privilege to do less

▶ freeing yourself from guilt and learning to stop

> planning ahead and making sure you schedule a day once a month, bi-monthly, quarterly even, to stop and do nothing but feed your soul!

Moments of recovery

I have – I like to think – a rich and varied life, ranging over family, business, career, writing, speaking and social commitments, and people have often said to me: 'I don't know how you do all you do.' My response is to tell them that I could not do it at all without silence, solitude and peacefulness woven deep into my everyday life. Full-blown retreats, quiet days, and silent beginnings and ends to my working days, provide me with the opportunity to recover, consolidate and better manage my time and energy. My zest for living and doing comes from a cradle of silence, solitude and deep concentration at the centre of my life. It provides an inner peacefulness from which I can draw the mental and physical energy that I require. It is the centre of the storm.

Moments of recovery and renewal of vigour are of as equal importance to full-on activity. It's something we could very easily teach children from an early age. Perhaps then we would respect its value in adulthood. A solid partnership of vigorous living and contemplative tranquillity should be at the heart of every life.

Key idea: A good warm-up

Busy modern living, frequently referred to as a 'treadmill', conjures images of endless pacing, with little choice but to continue along as it turns. It's an image that suggests that we are entirely passive victims of our circumstances, that the treadmill is something that happens *to* us and that our only reaction can be to take faster and faster steps. *But there is a choice!*

Just as it's foolish to do any vigorous exercise without a good warm-up first, it makes no sense to engage in unremitting activity without the quiet downtime that provides the energy and balance we need.

Traditionally, it was the holiday that provided us with the opportunity to renew our energies and to rejuvenate the mind and body, but today many holidays are characterized by a hyperactivity that if anything only compounds the anxious busyness of our everyday lives. The purpose of the holiday was originally to get away from it all, but now many people take 'it all' with them! The mobile phone and tablet go, too – thereby maintaining the connections to the places from which and the people from whom they were meant to be getting away.

But does even the traditional holiday truly serve its purpose? All too often the holiday is as jam-packed as our everyday lives. The holiday is just as much about achieving something – getting from A to B as quickly as possible to see the next famous must-see site – as work is. What we really need is a peacefulness that is woven into the rhythm of our workaday life, not reserved for a special occasion once a year, if we are lucky.

You may object that slowing down, stopping and reflecting in solitude, being more peaceful, is just for the mature in years, for those whose lives perhaps have been lived fast and who now need to ease up. But, in reality, peacefulness provides a balance that is necessary for all of us, if we want to live life well. Operating at optimum tilt can be fuelled by small quiet moments, rather like catnaps, scattered throughout our days, weeks, months, years. This rhythm provides healthy energy boosts on an ongoing process – far better, I'd argue, than any can of fizzy, performance-boosting drink!

Burn-out and recovery

The Olympic athlete would not expect to run race after race at top performance without taking time for recovery. The tennis star could not expect to uphold winning shots for the duration of a long match without short bursts of refreshment. During the long testing hours of a tennis match, concentration, composure and energy are maintained and fuelled by short periods of relaxation and contemplation. Only then can a top-class performance be delivered.

Today, though, we expect to skip moments of recovery in everyday life and still deliver full functionality and performance. Grabbing energy shots from caffeine-laden drinks seems an easier option than learning how to give ourselves concentrated moments of peacefulness. We dismiss regular moments of silent preparation or recovery as either a waste of time or as an unaffordable indulgence.

The body is designed with the capability to work hard physically and mentally, but this does not mean it can maintain full functionality without a respectful regard for its need to prepare itself and recover. Any mental or physical effort you put in to fulfil responsibilities in your work or home life requires preparation and recovery time. Left unappreciated or unattended to, levels of stress gradually build and back up, eventually overwhelming the system.

Taking action before this happens is the wisest move. Prevention rather than cure is the sensible solution. Our quick-fix culture usually means carrying on and expecting to fix things after they have broken. Peacefulness, however, is preventative – you make sure things don't get broken in the first place.

Case study

A head teacher once asked me to observe and assess a four-year-old girl's hyperactive behaviour and lack of concentration because these were having an effect on her classroom learning and her social interactions. My assessment was that she appeared to be 'over-stimulated'. With a little probing I discovered that she had a full menu of after-school activities every night of the week, in addition to the extra educational exercises that her parents gave her at home. Unsurprisingly, she was struggling to apply her full concentration in the classroom. She had no downtime, or recovery time, and was in a constant buzz.

Remember this: What's important?

Prepare and strengthen yourself by taking the time and the space to be alone and to review and reflect on what is important and what needs to be let go of. Notice how peacefulness rather than stress begins to seep into its place.

Silence amid the noise

As I was writing this, the peacefulness of my garden writing space was shattered by two men chopping down large trees just across the boundary of my home. Two chainsaws and then a helicopter and, further to this, a tractor working in the distance, broke the peaceful environment. Peacefulness has to be found in the thick of life, even when you live in the country!

It took a little while to realise how much I loved it. It was not a sudden plunge into solitude and silence; it was a gradual shifting of gears, a movement towards a new way of living that gave me an increasing deep satisfaction.

Sara Maitland, *A Book of Silence*

The difficulty many find when seeking peacefulness is the feeling of having little control over the noise and distraction that abounds externally in the world of work, home and life generally. We may seek to have a little peace and quiet, but noise, busyness and haste goes on around us, come what may.

Some try to find solace by finding a quiet place to live, but noise and demands are always present. They are just different. It is when ambient sounds and activity overwhelmingly distract you that opportunities for reflective and thoughtful thinking – for peacefulness – are scuppered.

Try to deselect ambient noise where you can. Don't go to a pub where the music blares out. Go to the shop where gentle music plays. Whenever you can, feed your soul with experiences that sooth. It will de-stress you. It is the attention paid to ambient sounds that steals inner silence, peacefulness. Silence is no longer golden, but stolen!

Case study

Csikszentmihalyi (2002) describes the role of peacefulness in the working life of a powerful and successful European woman, a scholar and businesswoman with an international reputation who clearly recognizes the essential part that peaceful solitude plays in helping her succeed in what she does – not by somehow escaping from distractions but by developing focus and redirecting attention towards inner composure and peacefulness. 'Each day... she devotes some time to recharging her mind, by such simple means as standing still for fifteen minutes on the lakeshore, facing the sun with eyes closed. Or she may take her hounds for a walk in the meadows on the hills outside town... She can disconnect her consciousness at will.'

Developing a sense of peacefulness is to find it, not in the *absence* of sound, but *amidst* it, so try to shut out the excess and look and listen beyond it.

Tapping into peacefulness even at busy moments is an invaluable tool in today's world, something that can boost our resilience in the face of even the most stressful times. It can be the key not just to a more balanced, less harried life, but, as we shall see, to success itself. High-achieving individuals and great thinkers alike have frequently recorded the merits of this ability to find calm in the storm, and point to it as the bedrock of success.

Try it now: Find peacefulness on a train

Next time you are on a train journey, resist the temptation to use your phone, laptop, tablet, or even to read a book for a while. If it is a long journey, try this for half an hour to an hour; if it's a short one, for the duration of the trip. Look out of the window instead. Observe and notice the passing landscape. Daydream. Note how you feel when you disembark.

Dissatisfaction and disquiet

Popular society breeds dissatisfaction and disgruntlement. Advertising encourages us to focus on what we don't have and preys on our insecurities and emotions. If we are not vigilant, we are subconsciously herded towards always seeking to aspire to something more. Perhaps human beings have always been motivated towards bettering their circumstances – in those prehistoric caves, warmer, safer, larger may well have been ongoing ambitions. It's on this basic human motivation, however, that modern marketing and advertising strategies seek to prey.

Remember when you first left your parental home? You were probably pretty content, managing reasonably well with a few basic possessions. I've listened often to people looking back to their earlier adult life in later years, reminiscing with respect and fondness for that time… 'Remember,' one couple reminisces, 'when all we had was that upturned tea chest as a table!'

Remember this: Be vigilant against marketing

Marketers deliberately build 'distress' elements into their pitches – an approach that causes us to worry about what might happen if we don't buy or do whatever it is they want us to do.

The answer is to be vigilant against such subliminal messages – against the 'have now, want now, do now, be now' culture. Think about what you truly need and want, then wait a little and think again. There is a value in waiting. It teaches us gratitude and moderation, and makes us less inclined to be greedy and always yearning for more.

Clearing the space for solitude

Whether you are a person who likes the company of others or not, you will more than likely recognize a need in your life for a little time to yourself. The way you approach this need will depend on how you value time in relation to both your mental and physical wellbeing.

So begin by reducing distractions. Create a 'stopping' space by actively working – mentally and physically – towards it:

CREATE THE MENTAL SPACE

▶ Determine to make a quiet time and recognize the *value* of what you are seeking.

▶ Turn down the *volume of thoughts* that drive you into action – let them pass by unnoticed.

▶ Give yourself *permission* to stop.

CREATE THE PHYSICAL SPACE

▶ Identify or create a *peaceful area* of your home/workplace where you are able to be alone for even just a short while, away from all distractions. It could be a spare room, a garden shed, or a quiet corner of a staffroom.

▶ If you can, display *meaningful or inspiring words and objects* in the space.

▶ Make sure *everyone knows* about the space and why it is sacrosanct.

Figure 2.1 A quiet corner of your home that can be yours for a while...

Try it now: Stress stopper

When you start to feel stressed during prolonged activity, try this little 'stress stopper':

* Become aware of yourself and take note of the stress and tension – and STOP!
* Become conscious of what is happening – remember you have allowed too much to build up.
* For a few seconds just stand or sit, and become aware of yourself again, your *being* rather than your *doing*.
* Take several deeper breaths and relax your shoulders.
* Take a short walk about if possible before returning to your desk or workstation.

You should now be in a more relaxed state. You should be calmer and your mind clearer. Be prepared to repeat the above steps, if you feel any residual tension or stress.

Focus points

* Take control of your own decisions.
* Think how you can achieve balance in all things.
* In terms of experiences, think 'quality, not quantity'.
* Be more selective as to how you spend your time.
* Seek peaceful opportunities throughout your day.

Moving on

You may have some questions at this point, such as:

* How can I stop myself from being over-committed?
* How do I reduce the pressure to succeed?
* How much time out from commitments is enough?
* I like my busy life – that can't hurt, can it?

Acknowledge that the busyness and commitments in your life have probably built up over a fairly long period of time. Just like a new fitness regime or weight-loss programme, you are more likely to recognize the benefits and succeed if you make small, incremental changes.

First, we'll take a look at the issue of our overcrowded lives and schedules from a new perspective.

3

Too Much to Be Good

In this chapter you will learn:

▶ *more about the effects of quantity and quality*
▶ *how to balance energy and time*
▶ *how to beat brain fatigue.*

Self-assessment

Before you begin this chapter, ask yourself the following questions:

1 How easy is it for me to relax?

2 How easy is it to get away for a holiday?

3 When I do get away, do I find it easy to disconnect and enjoy it?

4 Am I aware of just how many demands steal my peacefulness?

5 How competitively driven am I?

The overcrowded life

The great work of the solitary life is gratitude.

Thomas Merton

If you are seeking to maintain a healthy physical and emotional life and build realistic self-esteem, an overcrowded life can be counterproductive. Not only are there health and wellbeing issues at stake with the crowded life, such as the effects of stress and exhaustion, but there is the simple fact that the more we stuff into our lives the faster they appear to pass and the more we are forced to live them at a superficial level.

Crowding life with things and experiences, to the point of stress, is wasteful – of time, energy and opportunity. Relishing the flavours of life as they happen – enjoying the journey – leads to a richness and fulfilment that satisfy and causes us not to hunger greedily or desperately after having experiences. Quality replaces quantity. Just because we *can* does not necessarily mean that we *must*.

So why exactly do we fly in the face of common sense and cram our lives with half-baked and superficial experiences? The primary answer is *fear*.

Key dea: The valued life

Fast living is not valued living.

DRIVEN BY FEAR

Fear is both our friend and our enemy – it can both motivate and incapacitate. In origin, we know fear is linked to the primitive responses of fight or flight, and that it can help us to respond appropriately when a real threat comes our way. However, when fear is in the driving seat for too long it can have a debilitating effect. It becomes desperation – which destroys all our chances of finding peacefulness.

If any pressure reaches an overwhelming level, the fear of not managing, or coping well enough, creeps in and can have detrimental effects. The workload stacks up; we act faster, work harder; we employ more coping tactics, such as better time management or delegation and so on. The brain is in a pretty constant state of competitive drive, while the endocrine system, which controls our growth and development and our responses to our environment, works overtime to supply the energy and nutrition we need.

Eventually, though, without the proper recovery time and proper attention to the balance between mental and physical activity, tension, depression and general ill-health result. Our behaviour will become more aggressive, defensive and competitive, fuelled by testosterone and dopamine. The cycle of overwork and fear is locked into position. All too often, we come to accept that this is just the way things are and we persist in subjecting our minds and bodies to the burdens and stresses it imposes. It becomes a way of living without our fully appreciating the longer-term effects it has on our system.

People do not tend either to understand or to monitor themselves at these baseline physical levels. In fact, much of the socialization and early learning of humans teaches them to deny, project, repress, and hide their emotional responses to the world.

Richard R. Kilburg

So how do we know when too much is not good for us? Look out for the following 'symptoms' of an overcrowded life:

▶ Small things begin to irritate you as you worry that you won't keep up or achieve your goals.

- You are impatient with objects, situations and people, if they seem to threaten your endeavours.

- You are cutting corners in the hope that in that way you will be able to keep up.

- Your relationships with people around you are suffering, as you struggle incessantly for more space and time.

- You are become controlling and over-zealous.

Peacefulness seems a remote, and even irrelevant, feature in such a lifestyle. When the nose is against the wheel, it's not easy to see the complete picture. The whole vehicle and its direction of travel are obscured. This is when wrong decisions or actions are frequently taken. The mere idea of peacefulness is scorned as a waste of precious 'achievement time'.

But time out in solitude can do just that. It gives just that bigger picture and wider view missing in the overcrowded life. It can offer you the distance and perspective to see things as they really are and to make better-informed, well-considered decisions.

INATTENTION AND HYPERACTIVITY

Attention deficit and hyperactivity disorder (ADHD) is a condition often related to young children and their concentration and activity levels. Unable to attend to one task, person or situation around them for a protracted period of time, children are labelled with ADHD – their attention is said to be hyper-stimulated. High levels of inattention, impulsive behaviour and hyperactivity all form part of this condition. Worryingly, diagnosis of ADHD is on the rise in children.

Inattention increasingly affects adults, too. Many are hyper-distracted by the sheer amount of information that bombards us in modern life and rarely give anything or anyone their undivided attention. Information presents itself to us in the form of environmental signage and media out in the streets and through phones and computers, radio and television in the home as well.

We *try* to attend to it all, but the result is that we become increasingly *inattentive*.

Case study

The child looks up at his mother. She is sending the third text to her friend in the last ten minutes. And since a phone call with the same individual 15 minutes ago. The child seeks to meet her eye-to-eye. He tugs her cardigan. He wants her undivided attention for just a moment. He needs her to help him. But, sadly, she's communicating with someone elsewhere – someone virtually present, whom the child cannot see, but who nonetheless demands his mum's attention.

As a result of this distraction, his mother is not available to him. She is not fully present in the here and now. The here and now of this growing, enquiring child, who wants her attention right now, because... he has just found a fascinating creature and he doesn't know what it is. It intrigues and delights him and he wants to know what it is. Finally, Mum looks down from her handheld gadget and says impatiently, 'What, Jake? What do you want?' Jake tries to explain what he saw but it has already flown away. He'll have to wait for another chance to learn what a ladybird is; unless, of course, he happens to see a virtual one on a computer screen one day. Somehow not quite the same thing! And, anyway, Mum's looking back at her phone again...

Next time you are in a public area, look about you. Spot the mums, dads, adults who are present, but *not* present; adults with children beside them and their attention elsewhere. How must the modern world look to a three- or four-year-old? They look to us adults in the expectation of interaction and communication, because we are there at their side. However, with our heads tipped down and eyes fixed on a handheld screen, the child finds only a vacant presence!

The mobile phone is a wonderful communication tool, but it is also emblematic of our inattentive, hyperactive culture.

CLOCK-WATCHING

In today's world we are addicted to micro-measuring our time and obsessively counting the hours, minutes and seconds in which we have to do something. Time, however, is not the real issue – since we always have to make good use of it in relation to our energy. We talk about *time* management but really we should think more in terms of *energy* management. We can only do what we have the energy to do.

Humans in prehistoric times did not wear wristwatches. They had the same allotted hours in a day. They did not measure every millisecond and set out short, medium and long-term plans. They planted and reaped seasonally and worked in harmony with the rhythm of light and dark, sunrise and sunset. These were the parameters of the measurement of time.

Just because we can measure time so specifically and minutely in these current times does not mean that we actually should *always* do that.

Try it now: Don't wear a watch for a day

Try not wearing your watch for a day. Notice the differences in your behaviour.

Case study

'Without my watch I began to look for other clues, the angle of the sun, the habits of the birds, movements and behaviour of people – all these helped me guess. When I needed to know an exact time, I looked to a clock tower, or stopped someone in the street, which meant I was in human contact rather than digitally or mechanically distanced.'

Some antidotes to modern living

So, let's see how we can shake ourselves free from the binding compulsions of modern living – our overcrowded and overhasty lives:

▶ *Begin each day afresh.* It is a marvellous thing that we can begin every day afresh with new opportunities after a night's sleep. There's time before you to start all over again, even if yesterday was a disaster. At the beginning of every day, before you engage with it, consider that you have today a period of time between sunrise and sun set. Remind yourself of to what and to whom you have responsibility – family, neighbours, perhaps employer and wider society, and, of course, yourself. Think about the interrelationships between them and appreciate that one sacrificed at the expense of another leads to imbalance and stress, and ultimately away from the attainment of peacefulness.

▶ *Use time well.* Don't seek to gain time, or grieve at the loss of it. Respect it and it will be respectful to you. Let go of the pressure of being focused on the seconds and minutes, and stop micro-measuring every second, when you can.

▶ *Be attentive.* Practise being attentive by apportioning time between your responsibilities. Make sure that you consider, appreciate and give reverence to each part of your life every day.

▶ *Get into the habit of assessing and pondering the truth of what is really important to you in life.* Ask yourself if you really do *need* that new thing that's being dangled before you at the shops, on the Internet and on TV, in the magazines and newspapers. How much of your time and money will it in truth save? Is it worth the hassle to change, buy or maintain?

The antidote, above all, is to teach yourself peacefulness. Taking time out, not to rush and risk ensnarement, enables you to stand back and see all these messages for what they really are – an increasing assault on your time and, ultimately, your life.

Solitude helps you see the wood (the truth of successful living) despite the trees (the cultural myths about what constitutes a successful life). No longer will you burn with desire to have, but only with a burning desire for life. No longer will you covet the pursuits, status and belongings of others. Peaceful contentment grows in the soil of a nurtured and thoughtful awareness of reality.

Remember this: Be alert for envy

If you feel envious of others, then you have work to do in discovering the driving force that is motivating your envy. Also ask yourself whether the feeling is helping you or hindering you. Isn't it really breeding stress in your life rather than success in terms of peacefulness?

Reflective solitude acts like a kind of body scanner, helping you to detect the areas that challenge your peacefulness and motivate your desires and actions. It can facilitate your learning and lead you to want to help your neighbour, stand by friends, and build solid and genuine relationships, not to take offence and live defensively, despite what is thrown at you.

Those who have made the step, and gone through the gateway into solitude and found peacefulness, understand this well. The objectivity it provides is life-giving and life-sustaining.

Case study

My own experience of discovering the value of peacefulness began about 14 years ago when I was enduring a particularly difficult episode of work-related stress. I would go and sit at the bottom of my garden, under a tree and... just be! The time I spent doing this grew and grew, and it turned out to be a turning point in my life. Though there were difficult circumstances to navigate, a nugget of golden wisdom emerged in and through the silence.

The 'satisfaction circle'

Life today encourages dissatisfaction. Advertising can easily lead people into being dissatisfied with what they have, or what they don't have. Constantly changing fashions and fads drive dissatisfaction, which in turn breeds more consumer desire and more dissatisfaction. Your goal should be to replace dissatisfaction with its opposite. Look at the diagram below:

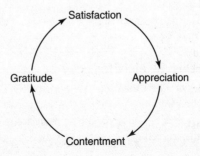

Satisfaction leads to appreciation, appreciation to contentment, and gratitude then completes the circle.

Try it now: Get gratitude

Make a list of all the things you are truly grateful for at this moment in time.

One way of becoming more satisfied with your life is to engage more with what you are doing in the here and now. Given that we are encouraged to want to take the satisfaction out of things we do and have and to aspire to everything that is remote from our workaday lives, you might like to begin by reacquainting yourself with the 'ordinary'. You may think that there is more to be had from life than washing up, or washing the car, or doing a spot of weeding – tasks that we are inclined to dismiss as a 'waste' of time and energy, preventing us from doing 'real', more important things – but think again!

Looking back at the purpose of such tasks helps you to value their importance in their own right. They may seem like mundane, mindless jobs, but you'd be surprised at how a mundane exercise can help you relax and become peaceful if you let it. If your only objective is to get a clean car or clean dishes, then you will not gain any satisfaction from it. However, if you value the task *itself* and know that by dong it you are making a contribution to a peaceful, reflective time and getting a good job done at the same time, you will gain satisfaction.

Case study

A few years ago on a cruise down the Nile I remember seeing mothers and children at the edge of the river as we sailed past. The women were singing as they did their washing in the running water and they seemed very satisfied and engaged with what they were doing. A mundane task had given them a few moments of peaceful contentment.

Valuing the task in hand, not rushing away, either in thought or action, allows you to 'stay in the moment' and reap from it what it intrinsically holds. Rather than have your mind rush off to somewhere, or something, else, take the time to value it. Take time over:

- making breakfast

- looking into a loved one's eyes at a mealtime

- writing with a fountain pen rather than a Biro

- talking face to face over a coffee with a friend, not via a social network site

- mowing the lawn slowly, then sitting back to admire it.

When your final hour comes, will you be glad that you lived life at top speed, or that you appreciated it for its quality experiences?

The role of technology

What matters more – speed or quality? The Biro enabled speedier writing, and the quality of script mattered less. Perhaps this was the beginning of a depreciation of handwriting as an art form. I guess there's an argument for both, but in any pursuit of peacefulness, quality is more important.

Now we have word processing, things are even speedier. Certainly, there is no calm filling of ink or placing of nib, just the repetitive strain caused hammering away at a keyboard. I was taught handwriting at school and the physical posture to go with it – a relaxed position with elbows supported and fingers gently gripping the fountain pen. Writing was indeed treated like an art – keeping the ink from dribbling on to your fingers and page indiscriminately certainly was anyway!

We don't even need keyboards now, because we have speech recognition software. Technology is in constant progression, yet what is lost in the process?

Recently, watching a documentary about the Romans, I discovered that a significant amount of knowledge about the lives of ordinary people in Rome has been gleaned because chiselled into stone – specifically gravestones – were stories and snapshots of the lives of individual people – a real treasure trove carved in rock for us to read and marvel at. Tombstones have since been superseded by the mass use of paper, Biro and now computer technology, but I'm not so sure that people thousands of years from now will learn very much about us – as individuals – from the hasty records that we create.

I'm not advocating that we all go back to inscribing stones in order to send a letter – a small paper envelope costs enough to post! What I *am* saying is that the slow, considered art forms of ancient times have created something of enduring value and are deeply resonant of peace and contemplation. The hypnotic states that screen culture promotes may *seem* like peacefulness, but it is not of the healthy kind. Eyes stare, the posture is fixed, and the muscles are tense... Screen technology can have even more insidious effects, however.

A book written by Martin Large in the 1980s, *Who's Bringing Them Up?*, pointed out the effects of television viewing on children, and by extension on adults, too, at a time when satellite TV and the commercialization of television channels were only just beginning to emerge, at least in the UK. Drawing on worldwide research into the subject, Large spoke of the hypnotic effects that the TV screen itself had on the brain, let alone the content of what actually was being viewed. The addictive nature of viewing means that we are regularly plugging in for a hypnotic fix:

Observe people viewing – the 'television stare', the fixed position of the eyes and head, the minimal movement of the eyes – which take in the whole screen in a slightly de-focused way. By contrast in normal vision, the eyes are continually moving and focusing.

Martin Large, *Who's Bringing Them Up?:
How to break the TV habit*

What's more, television commercials exploit to the maximum the fact that we are in a semiconscious state when we are watching TV, making us even more vulnerable to the power of advertising.

When we consider how many more types of screen there are in the average household today, we can see how the inimical effects of screen culture seem to be multiplying.

Try it now: Ignore that TV... if you can!

Next time you are near a television set:

* Try ignoring it when you walk into a room, pub or waiting area where it is switched on;
* Try and notice how you respond to it. *Can* you ignore it? Make a point of sitting with your back to it and see what difference that makes.

You will probably note that in a fairly short time you find yourself drawn to look at the screen. You will be grabbed by the sound, but mostly by the images; the movement atracts our primeval attention receptors. Try turning the volume down and see if that makes any difference to whether you are drawn to the screen or not.

Beat brain fatigue

Making small solitary steps away from the fray of modern living can work wonders in terms of providing perspective, inspiring extra enthusiasm, motivating change, and enabling you to see things in their true form. Best of all, such steps increase your sense of gratitude for the life you are living. Just like some atmospheric fog insidiously creeping in and swirling around you, the way we have lived in the past 50 to 60 years or so has generated a climate of fear, envy, dissatisfaction and unhappiness. It has made people talk badly of others in order to feel better themselves, and to live out their ambitions through the lives of their children, their status and material possessions. This may in part be 'human nature', but, if so, it is a nature that modern marketing exploits and preys upon.

People who have taught themselves peacefulness have begun a journey into transcending the need to prove, impress and seek to blind others with the superficial. Giving the over-stimulated and fatigued mind a much-needed rest, we are en route to genuinely fulfilling lives.

Remember this: Give things time

Combat our culture of immediate gratification by giving things time to gestate – attending to and learning peacefulness allows you to see that some things are simply *not* required while others are truly worth treasuring and nurturing.

Focus points

✳ Value time, rather than measuring – and bewailing – the lack of it.

✳ Attentiveness gives rewards to others as well as yourself.

✳ Satisfaction in life is not about finding more opportunities, but finding it where you are right now.

✳ Tune in to the real effects that TV viewing is having on you and your family.

✳ Perspective is gained from distance.

Next step

You may have some questions at this point, such as:

✳ **How can being alone help me better value time?**
✳ **How can I get the head space I need?**
✳ **How can solitude reduce stress?**
✳ **Will I be able to cope with silence?**

These are all questions that many people put to me when they first think about quiet and solitary time. Yes, it *is* a challenge, especially within the context of our modern ways of living, but, as we shall see in the next chapter, understanding silence is the first step to learning how to be alone...

4

The Value of Silence

In this chapter you will learn:

- ▶ *about the value of personal silence*
- ▶ *how to identify opportunities for silence*
- ▶ *about solitude and professional success.*

Self-assessment

Before you read this chapter, ask yourself these self-assessment questions:

1 What does silence mean to you?

2 When do you experience silence?

3 How comfortable are you with silence?

4 How might solitude prepare you for stressful situations?

5 Could silence energize you?

Personal silence

Talent develops itself in solitude; character in the stream of life.
Johann Wolfgang Goethe, *Maxims and Reflections*

Why is silence important to us? Apart from being a respite from the noise that calls us to involvement, silence can also 'speak', communicating through *absence* of sound. The silent pauses between notes in music create rhythm that speaks to us in different ways. Fast and slow rhythms are made richer and stronger when silent pauses intersperse them. Silence keeps us in anticipation and expectation. A good storyteller uses silent pauses to create suspense.

Silence can help us tune back in with sensitivity to the world around us, reawakening our primeval alertness to environmental changes, ears pricked, eyes sharpened. It is for this reason that silence can also make us fear the unknown. There are certain sounds we expect to hear, like the birds singing and traffic humming. When there is sudden absence of these expected sounds, we feel suspicious. Why have the birds stopped singing, when they usually would be?

Sometimes we long for real silence, but we usually only want it when we expect it or create it for ourselves. We are unused, in a modern world, to really experiencing the sound of silence.

How to do we turn down the volume? Creating the pause between the endless beats of an active 'noisy' life is the first step.

The tornado is a useful metaphor here. Creating silent spaces, the eye of the storm, at the centre of the raging storm of life that encircles us. The two are held in balance, the one enclosed within, not at some distant place from the other. Peacefulness and silence can be integral. Feelings and emotions, activity and demands, may twist and turn around the centre, but silence can be held serenely within, not ensnared.

Silence is rather like a volume-less call to us from the other side of the wall of noise. We often don't hear it and as a consequence we get caught in the surrounding storm instead of responding peacefully. It can be ignored. We won't suffer too much without it, not in the short run anyway. Therefore we save silence for a rainy day. When there's time for it. When there's nothing much else going on. And, of course, there rarely is such a time. Engaged in the lives of our friends and family, occupied with work, hobbies and interests, the silent call is ignored. We are pulled into the storm.

Remember this: A brief silence

A peaceful state is not easy to reach amid the fuggy atmospheres of noise and hubbub. Yet silence even for a short while, just like the momentary musical pause, creates a mental space that refreshes and invigorates the harmony of mindfulness and efficient thinking.

Silence is the starting place of the journey to peacefulness, enabling you to listen to who you are and your place in the world. Silence and peacefulness may seem such small and seemingly insignificant values in the wider scheme of personal endeavour, but their impact can be huge.

Silence is multifaceted, a densely woven fabric of many different strands and threads.

Sarah Maitland, *A Book of Silence*

The power of silence

Quiet, or silent, approaches are often more powerful than loud or aggressive ones. The practice of horse whispering is a great example of how the quiet approach can be fruitfully used,

Figure 4.1 The peaceful silence found in solitude, especially in the midst of the natural world, can be both restful and empowering.

in this instance to reassure a wild or defensive animal. Similarly, in the face of adversity an active kind of silence can be immensely powerful. An action speaks louder than a word so often. Thinking more about what *not* to say is sometimes more pertinent. Words can harm and make a difficulty worse.

The wonderful event in 2008 when a couple of hundred people froze motionless for five minutes in Grand Central Station, New York City, is one such example of the power of silence. No words were spoken. Their silence spoke loudly to millions. There was a sense of anti-climax when normal movement and activity resumed. Silence frequently has more impact than a grand fanfare.

Similarly, to practise sitting in silence, alone, from time to time helps us to turn down the volume in our busy and overcrowded lives. It *is* possible to learn to still the many thoughts and anxieties which try to buzz into your head and steal your silence at such times. By hijacking, intercepting and stopping thoughts as they arise, as soon as they enter the mind, and conversely by replacing them with a single word or idea, we can tame our hyperactive brains.

Try it now: Hold your position

Try stopping right now. Be silent. Quietly look out of the window. Pause in silence. Do nothing but wait inside that silence. What happens? Usually, because we are not used to it, the mind wanders into thinking, worrying, and so on. 'Gosh! The lawn is getting long. It needs a cut. When am I going to get time to do that this week? I have a dentist appointment later...' If, at the point of noticing the long grass, you dwell instead on its richness of green, on the daisies and buttercups, the beauty of it, irrespective of whether it needs cutting, you keep your mind in the moment of pleasure and ignore the temptation of falling into anxious and worrying thoughts.

Similarly, you may use a word or phrase to yourself to hijack those run-away thoughts. This could be something like 'I'm resting and enjoying the peace', 'I love the green grass. It makes me restful'. Or repeat one word, such as 'beauty' or 'freedom' over and over inside your head. *Tell yourself before* you take your moment of silence that you will have concentrated time *afterwards* to think about all the jobs you have to do, and have a pen and paper ready. But don't do it before – you will have primed the brain to automatically trawl for more things you need to do while you are having a moment of quiet.

Practised regularly for just 15 minutes every day, this can become a deeply rewarding experience. Gradually, it becomes easier. You learn to sit inside the silence, in the present moment, and be mindful of yourself, without others around to distract you. It is rather like a preparation before being with others again. It reduces striving, hurry and pressing agendas. It helps you to let go and *let be* a little more. It provides something of an antidote to our pressured modern world – inner knowledge, respect and even humility begin to emerge.

It can also be valuable to do with a partner or spouse. Sitting companionably without words is a profoundly enriching experience. A mutuality of respect and understanding develops and an experience is shared.

Sitting awhile with ourselves, and without the noise and hum of perpetual responsibilities and demands, both sooths the hastened mind and offers a wealth of peacefulness that supports and assists us when we are again in the company of others. More is learned about self in silence. It is where we reflect on the interactions we have and the roles they play in our lives; it is where we gain insight into what might be a more considered and realistic life as well as fresh momentum.

Try this: Use silence to find your values

Next time you have time in silence, reflect on and note down what your personal values are about silence. List them. Think about them. Think about how they are concretely reflected in the way you choose to live.

As we have noted, silence is not just an auditory experience; it can be highly visual, too. We even see or touch things that have a silent quality about them, a peacefulness. Looking at a beautiful photograph of a frozen moment in time, or standing under a majestically silent oak tree, we realize that these things have a presence that feeds our peacefulness. Take time for these moments. Five minutes every day can be all that is needed to encourage peacefulness.

Aloneness and togetherness

Alone and lonely are two separate experiences:

▶ *Loneliness* is a craving for company and attention;

▶ *Aloneness* is the simple act of not being engaged socially, of being physically or psychically detached.

We need times alone to complement social time. We can find peacefulness with the inner person we are, our soul, when time is planned and taken alone. Alone with our thoughts and ideas, our needs and feelings, we begin to appreciate and understand the person we are, and who we have the potential to become as we develop and grow. In oneness, we find ourselves.

We are, of course, designed as social animals. To a greater or lesser degree, we enjoy and also grow through the company of others. Just as a field of poppies stands together as one beautiful spectacle, each stem of each flower, each root of each plant, also stands alone within the crowd and requires its own nourishment to survive and flourish. Togetherness is where we reflect who we are within different spheres of interaction. Alone (in solitude) we familiarize ourselves with the person we are on the inside; with others, what we give to the outside.

Peacefulness is disturbed if social interaction drowns out our oneness. We need to re-engage with the stem of our personal unique existence now and again; our successful development and survival depend upon it. So, stand back for a while, without heeding the views and comments of others. Reflect on who you are and what defines you, before and after you commune with others. It builds silent strength and counters stress.

The best way to balance your life demands is to acknowledge that you need both time alone and time with others. You become the person you are meant to be by respecting both needs in your life. This forms the basis of many spiritual and religious practices: the ability to be both alone and together with others, even simultaneously, can foster a deep spirituality and a fruitful life. It is this seemingly paradoxical juxtaposition that lies at the heart of the monastic ideal, for example.

We can find similar interdependent rhythms of opposites in many areas of natural life – day and night; sun and moon, the movement of the tides; winter dormancy and summer fruitfulness. These are the rhythms of growth and decline, progression and regression. The value and benefit of each opposite are obvious when we see them working one with the other in a rhythm of completeness. One without the other cannot be sustained. We require the tension of opposites to achieve a rich and fruitful life.

Stress and silence

It is well understood that stress can be good in getting us up out of the chair and motivating us to the achievement of our desires, plans and goals. Its downside is that too much stress becomes negative and counterproductive when we are driven by it.

The demands of work, responsibilities and dependencies become too high and too hard to handle, and create situations where we feel overwhelmed, fearful and exhausted.

Silence provides an opportunity to prepare for stress as well as recover from it. If time alone in quiet personal reflection is scheduled regularly into life, it helps to offset stressful demands. For some, physical solitude may be itself stressful, initially. When the habit of being around others all the time is strong, it feels like an alien experience. In order to get the best from solitude, first get used to a little silence. The practice of nourishing solitude is better broken into small steps.

What does the silence tell you?

Especially if you are unused to silence, you may believe that standing alone, sitting alone, just being alone, does not specifically *say* anything at all. Receiving information through engagement and interaction with people and various communication channels gives you more directional signals, surely? Yet, if you are prepared to listen to the inner thoughts and feelings within yourself, you will begin to notice an instinctive channel of wisdom perpetually guiding your footsteps.

Key idea: Silence and reason

More reasoned thought comes from silent reflection.

Whether you have a positive or negative outlook on life, it is possible to listen honestly to personal beliefs hidden within the unconscious self. These parts of the person you are tend to be quietened when you are in company, though they do unconsciously affect your relationships, decisions and actions around others.

Silence and solitude tell us many things about the reality of ourselves with regard to what motivates our actions, the situations we face and our lifestyle choices. As we get in touch with the inner self, we discover truths that speak out about what we are really feeling and what we really need. When trying to cope with an enormous pressure or a life-changing situation, such as a job change or becoming a dad or mum for the first time, silence can reveal hidden difficulties and tensions, some of which may require talking through with a friend, or a trained mentor, coach or counsellor.

Remember this: Solitude can lead to honesty

Solitude can be enlightening when you let it reveal the reality of the situations you face. It enables you to be more honest with yourself – you do not have to put on the brave face you do for others.

By talking with friends or counsellors you can reflect on what you hear and experience in solitude, weighing this against your beliefs and values as a framework for finding truth and your own conviction. It can help to reinforce what you need to do, and sometimes to put you in touch with changing aspects of your personality and your needs. It might, for example, tell you that you *must* slow down. It might tell you that it is OK to take on the risk of a new opportunity...

Case study

I knew that one of my values in life was to live simply, without causing harm. Yet, when I stopped and really thought about some of my actions, I realized that they actually ran counter to this value. I had no idea I was being hypocritical. Now I try to live a life that is more consistent with my values.

Solitude and consolidation

I view solitude as an opportunity for consolidation. We do not learn well if we do not stop to think about how that learning works with, or applies to, other things and experiences. This is consolidation. We otherwise become stuffed full of discrete thoughts and ideas without gaining a true insight into, and perspective on, the whole. We are at risk of being rather easily conditioned if we do not take time to distil the facts, ideas and suggestions put to us.

In silence, thoughts are distilled, affirmed or dismissed and either assigned to memory or not. We witness this in children. When a very young child is told 'This is a dog', in silence he reflects and recalls other times when he has seen a four-legged, hairy animal with two long ears and a tail. He consolidates this knowledge and distils it down until he knows there are differences between four-legged, furry animals. Some are, in fact, cats, others horses and so on. He silently ponders before accepting or dismissing knowledge. Silently, he builds up a picture of the world around him born of this consolidation time within his solitary world of understanding. If he were to rush on, gathering new information without solitary reflection, he would be left with gaps that would later make him vulnerable to misunderstanding.

Missing out on consolidation time means missing out on the vital parts in the development of understanding and ultimately the growth of wisdom.

Silence and professional success

The working and business worlds are fast-paced places these days. We may not immediately associate silence, solitude or peacefulness with such environments, but in fact they can help with the discovery of true identity and potential in the workplace. This may feel like scary stuff to the not so intrepid, but digging deep into what actually defines and excites you is important. Needs, hopes and fears become more obvious in the silence of our solitude, and the route to true potential can be more easily formed and followed.

A more disciplined and structured approach to periods of silent reflection should not be seen as a chore or as a waste of time, but rather as an opportunity. It offers us time to reflect on and review our working life outside the usual professional boundaries. Reflective space can be a valuable professional tool therefore, especially when dealing with people or difficult situations at work. Perspective is gained as complex issues are dealt with, leading to perceptive and insightful practice.

In demanding working environments we require intuition, insight and a creative perspective, particularly when we work closely with others. Creative problem-solving in challenging situations is more likely to be achieved with a little quiet reflection scheduled into our agenda. A quiet thinking space would be a valuable resource in every workplace – somewhere inspiring that encourages relaxation and silent reflection. Not only would this be a place for recovery, but a hothouse for creativity.

In business, as elsewhere, when decisions depend on the use of faint clues in intricate situations, the tortoise outstrips the hare.
Guy Claxton, *Hare Brain Tortoise Mind*

Case study

Steve had been a successful senior manager for many years. When he began to find that things seemed to be getting too much for him, he tried to keep going, despite feeling increasingly stressed. He was mindful of the responsibilities he had to his staff and his family, and this, for a time, kept him going. Eventually, though, he fell ill.

After a period of several months away from work, he gradually realized where he had gone wrong. He had been trying to maintain the high standards he expected of himself while ignoring an inner need to do something different, to go in a different direction. That small 'voice' that had been nudging him for some while could really only be heard once he had stopped.

Focus points

✳ Alone and lonely are two very different things: alone can be powerful, lonely not so.
✳ Try to take silent breaks from work or at home.
✳ Learn to appreciate silence.
✳ Find things that help you to be silent – a picture, a piece of music, etc.
✳ Silent reasoned thought is helpful when dealing with people – in social relations as well as business.

Moving on

You may have some questions at this point, such as:

✳ What do I do if I feel uncomfortable with silence?
✳ It might be silent on the outside, but why am I still buzzing on the inside?
✳ What if silence makes me feel even more stressed?
✳ How do I make solitude happen for me?

Silence is not something we are so familiar with in our modern culture. Noise rules! But by giving silence a chance to assert itself, on a more regular basis, you begin to realize its value. As you do so, you will notice that you can afford to kick your heels a little and still not lose track or miss out on the action. You will begin to notice, and learn to enjoy, peacefulness, while at the same time not sacrificing productivity...

5

Creating Peacefulness

In this chapter you will learn:

- ▶ *about making moments of deliberate solitude*
- ▶ *about the importance of play and taking your time*
- ▶ *about what facilitates peacefulness for you.*

How do you feel?

Before you begin this chapter ask yourself the following questions:

1 How much thought do you give to valuing your time?

2 What do you prioritize in your life?

3 How much do your routines drive you, rather than you driving them?

4 What hobbies and interests do you have?

5 When do you feel fully attentive to the situations that arise in your life?

Making moments of deliberate solitude

A series of psychological studies over the past twenty years has revealed that after spending time in a quiet rural setting, close to nature, people exhibit greater attentiveness, stronger memory, and generally improved cognition. Their brains become both calmer and sharper.

Nicholas Carr, *The Shallows*

The true antidote to technologically governed, fast-paced or over-committed living is more time and connection with the natural world, not just doing less. For a sharper, more efficient brain, we need the inner silence and peacefulness that connection with the natural environment offers. Whether it's a hike in the open countryside, a walk in the park, or just a saunter through your garden, connecting with nature points us towards an inner peacefulness and contentment, if we engage fully and mindfully.

The difficulty, of course, is the more disconnected we become from the natural world, the more indifferent, or lazy, we become at seeking it out and enjoying it. But look at the benefits – greater attentiveness, cognition and stronger memory, as Nicholas Carr points out. Moments of deliberate solitude, noticing and connecting with the environment, help balance the interrelationship between sharper and slower thinking. The mind becomes tuned to the inner self in relation to the outer.

Try it now: Connect with nature

Walk out into your garden now, or go to your local park. Be still for a moment and concentrate on some small aspect of the natural world – a flower, the branch of a tree, a butterfly. How does that make you feel?

If we *prime* ourselves with thoughts and ideas of peacefulness, by integrating deliberate moments of silence and solitude into our busy lives, our chances for contentment and satisfaction will be increased.

The key thing I firmly believe is making a *deliberate* choice. Don't leave it to chance. If you deliberately seek out solitude, there is more chance of you finding inner silence and peace. Becoming aware of, and practising, silence, peacefulness and solitude, as separate but interrelated states, we begin to recognize and understand the golden thread that runs between them. This thread represents the contentment that is felt as peacefulness comes within.

Seeking solitude

Solitude is often something we only ever experience for odd moments of time, during those ten minutes in the shower, or while walking to the bus stop alone. For others, who perhaps live alone, they may find they have too much of it. It is worth taking stock of how often you spend truly alone, in solitude, during the course of a day. It may be you rarely ever experience it. Once you have identified how often you are truly alone, consider how you respond to it. Do you welcome it? Do you hate or fear it? Do you reject it?

Case study

When the kids were small I used to long for just five minutes on my own, without anyone around me. But on the odd occasion when it did happen, I didn't know what to do with myself. It was as though I'd lost myself. What I wanted, what I needed, was crowded out by everyone else's needs and demands. I never really knew whether to sit and chill with a coffee and a magazine, which, I have to say, seemed a bit selfishly indulgent, or whizz round doing a few jobs that were harder when the children were about. Just doing *nothing* didn't feature as an option. I quite literally didn't know how to deal with the solitude. So I'd ring a friend and catch up!

However you view solitude, it is important make it work *for* you rather than *against* you. Time out alone facilitates a rerun through events, for example at the end of the day, or as preparation time for the coming day. Developing an inner peacefulness through these times, thoughts and experiences are consolidated and reinforced. In turn, this assists memory and brain function. As we have seen, fast living without good recovery periods over time reduces the ability to cope and maintain a demanding life.

Small 'breathing spaces' in which to do nothing but listen and relax alone provide clarity, perspective and possibility. You value and respect the importance of such states and times, you will reap many short- and longer-term benefits for your mental health and wellbeing, as well as personal, even professional, developmental opportunities. More creativity, entrepreneurial spirit, wisdom, and inspired objectivity may be just a few of the many by-products.

Remember this: Be gentle with yourself

The wise words of Max Ehrmann's well-known 'Desiderata' speak of being 'gentle with yourself'. What he means by this is not to wrap yourself in cotton wool, seeking to avoid every difficulty or disappointment that life sends, or being affronted when adversity does happen, but to strengthen yourself through a healthy self-discipline that gently takes care of your human needs. This builds the strength and vitality you need to live with the highs and lows of life more objectively.

Try some of the following ideas to help you let go of some of the battling demands of everyday living:

▶ Spend a day – or even just an hour – without any kind of technology. Changing your ideas about how available you are to contact by phone, email, social networking and so on can be life-transforming.

▶ Try not use the phone for 24 hours – prime others and say you will not be available.

- Do not read a newspaper for a couple of weeks, or don't take one every day of the week.

- Tune yourself to good news.

- Are those TV soaps really that appealing? Are you addicted to them? Try turning the TV off for at least one night a week and listen to music instead.

These are just a few small changes, but you may be surprised by the significant effects they can bring about by you making them.

Case study

Most frustrations are born of our will to push certain things along in a way *we want* them to or *believe* they should go. I have learned that most things do not really matter as much as I perceive them to do. We have enough to manage and deal with in ordinary life today, without generating more stress for ourselves.

An example for me has been the Internet connection in the garden cabin where I write. It behaves sporadically and could be a great focus of stress and frustration to me, particularly when I have a good deal of work to get through. I have learned to live with it and now see it as a bonus when it works, but beneficial even when it does not, as I am less tempted to distract myself and so get more done! The distractions of surfing the Net or checking emails, even shopping, have all been removed from under my nose. It helps me to be more focused and disciplined. I attend solely to the job in hand and therefore experience deeper satisfaction.

Time out

KICK YOUR HEELS AND BE PLAYFUL AGAIN

Children do it easily. Playing is their learning *for* life. Many adults perceive playing as a frivolous thing or the domain only of children. Playing is for those who are not really living! Having a full schedule and doing something all the time mean you're not wasting a minute of life to idleness. However, while playfully 'kicking your heels' now and again may seem like a luxury, in fact it can be an invaluable de-stressor. And, at times of having 'nothing else to do' your brain is allowed the necessary space to drift a little.

To experience the kind of self-satisfaction and achievement that stems from inner peacefulness, we need to harmonize a range of human ambitions and endeavours in work, relationships and leisure. Csikszentmihalyi (in *Flow: The classic work on how to achieve happiness*) describes these as 'flow experiences' – the times when we feel that our challenges and skills are synchronized and balanced within these spheres of life to the point of self-contentment. It becomes effortless action. Play is frequently one such activity.

Even when we do not experience this state fully, harmonizing what we believe and value with what we do provides greater contentment. Cultivating a habit of taking time to be playful and for recreation, particularly in a full-on working life, provides us with an opportunity to explore other areas of life where there is more chance of flow. This might be in solitude or in company, or both!

There is quite extensive evidence showing that even if one does not experience flow, just the fact of doing something in line with ones goals improves the state of mind.

Mihaly Csikszentmihalyi, *Flow: The classic work on how to achieve happiness*

REAWAKEN THE CHILD WITHIN YOU

Curiosity is an innate aspect of human nature. Head and heart are engaged together in the drive to find out, explore and experiment. Think of the very young child, as she totters into the world. From day one she 'plays' with the possibilities of sound, light, dark, warmth, touch and smell. She experiments with what things do and how things are done. She explores what does and doesn't work in the world beyond self and how it relates to herself. All the time she gathers and re-gathers data, enabling her to reflect and recheck until she acquires frames of reference, or schema, that help her towards understanding.

We are *still* that child, though admittedly grown into further complexity through our experiences and the influences of conditioning. We take much for granted now. We have, after all, seen it before. We have assigned much to the vaults of the unconscious mind. Taking time for rechecking the data does not seem as critical as when we were children. We now make assessments at the drop of a hat. There is little time, in our activity-filled lives, to stop and think and spend a little time pondering. We believe we have amassed all the knowledge we really need about the world and now our assumptions are fixed, like some grand old edifice, built upon all our prior experiences.

How, then, can we reawakening the sleeping child within us? Childlike curiosity, wonder and the impelling drive for living are reawoken when, in solitude, we start to explore and take real notice again, without the confining prisons of cynicism, familiarity, scepticism and prejudice.

Case study

The young child was walking with his granddad around the garden. Granddad was looking at the weeds that were invading the lawn and thinking about how he would find time to grub them out. The child was pointing out every daisy, every buttercup, bee and butterfly, he spotted.

Time in peaceful aloneness, or solitude, can help to rebuild curiosity and wonder, by giving us the opportunity to recheck the data – our feelings, experiences and assumptions – and to add new and exciting possibilities to what was previously understood. Everything is continually and subtly changing, so we must adapt and change in similarly subtle ways. This is, after all, the excitement and challenge of life.

APPRECIATION

There is little time set aside these days to appreciate and be thankful for what we have and what we enjoy. When we drift a little, play a little and enjoy what we have now, and do not stress over what we have *not* got, then we can more likely appreciate our life and show gratitude for it. Every six months or so, during times alone, I write down all the good things in my life. It is amazing how much changes and how this builds gratitude and contentment.

The further I advance into solitude the more clearly I see the goodness of things.

Thomas Merton, *No Man Is an Island*

LINGER LONGER

Even in very basic activities such as personal hygiene, we can find opportunities for peacefulness. Nowadays we are used to taking a quick shower rather than a long bath. Showers may be cleaner, more energy-efficient, but the mind misses an opportunity for relaxation and reflection. Past generations took baths. They reused the water, so were not as wasteful of resources as we might think! The experience of soaking in warm water, with time to relax, is a restorative and reflective experience that many of us have ditched in our quest for faster living.

Try it now: Take a bath!

Try taking a bath once a week, even once a month – in between your showers, of course! Unlike a shower, it will increase your time to be alone, if you linger a while. Away from all distractions, a bath is an opportunity to do nothing but lie back and soak up the physical pleasures of warm water lapping at your body. The refreshing combination of stillness and warmth both relaxes and refreshes the body and mind. Cleansing the body has a cleansing effect on the mind. Significant thoughts or inspired ideas come to the surface; tension-induced ones are let go. Thoughts get distilled as you linger.

Many people, when asked where they usually get their best ideas or solutions to problems, say that is when they are alone in the bath. Your mind has the time to drift and ideas that have been fragmentary or discrete suddenly coalesce and take shape. Even a slightly longer shower than usual can have similar effects. Take your time!

Case study

I always start my day with a long shower. It seems to put me straight for the day, providing me with not only a fresh physical feeling, but also a mental readiness. The thinking time this affords has to a degree replaced the walk to work I used to do years ago – a period when I would think about the day ahead and mentally prepare as I walked.

The power of the bath or shower enables us to access the realm of 'slower thinking'. In his book *Hare Brain Tortoise Mind*, the professor of psychology Guy Claxton discusses the characteristics of slower and faster thinking, and emphasizes the importance of *intuition* and *inspiration* in the slower kind. 'It is not just that people are bolder about trying things out when they feel relaxed and secure,' he writes, 'threat creates a mind-set of anxiety and entrenchment in which awareness is constricted and focused on the avoidance of the threat, rather than the spacious, open attitude that the slow ways of knowing require to work.'

TRY BEING BORED OR DAYDREAMING NOW AND THEN

I know it sounds rather crazy, but experiencing a relative feeling of boredom from time to time can be more productive than it sounds. It provides your brain with a breathing space, one that it may need for the kind of thinking that allows the creative juices to flow – not just an artistic variety of creativity, but the kind that promotes fresh ideas, finds solutions and induces conceptual inspiration. Interestingly, the Greek word for 'leisure' is *scholea*, the root of our words 'school' and 'scholar' – an etymology that neatly encapsulates the idea that leisure can lead us towards knowledge and understanding.

Being in a 'brown study', or reverie, means to daydream, to be in a state of deep absorption and thoughtfulness. It can have a negative inference if it looks like we're simply wasting our time away aimlessly. But when we step back, stand away for a while, we find the voice of who we really are. We tune our ear to the possibilities of thought and ideas within our daydreams. Artists, writers, designers – all manner of people who manufacture original and creative works from an amalgam of experiences – find that time 'away' brings a bountiful flood of fresh ideas and perspectives. We are not wasting time, but giving the brain much needed quality thinking space.

Key idea: The value of daydreams

Daydreaming, drifting off into a dream while awake, often has a negative connotation. We have probably been conditioned to wake up, sit up and look alert. Daydreaming suggests a 'switching off', with nothing much going on in the brain. Yet it can very often be a time when thoughts are consolidated and ideas discovered. Daydreaming is not the waste of time you might think; it can lead to great achievements.

Charles Handy, in a study of successful entrepreneurs, found a common denominator between a diverse mix of successful and visionary individuals, such as Richard Branson – this was the ability to 'dream in the daytime'. Using the power of the daydream, these people were able to visualize ideas and pinpoint opportunities with such clarity that they were also able to muster the strength, determination and resources to turn them into realities.

So, allowing yourself to daydream and mindfully drift away can be rewarding – a seedbed of potential and opportunity. By holding on to the idea of avoiding daydreaming, never allowing yourself to be bored, you may be missing out on some creative entrepreneurialism or, at the very least, on a chance to discover ways and opportunities for enriching your own life.

Case study

'I was often "caught" daydreaming as a child. I'm sure it caused much irritation to the people around me, the teachers or family members who wanted my full attention. Yet I felt most in tune with myself at those times. I would be in a world of ideas, thoughts and ponderings. Now, as an adult, I have come to value these times. Know it's my best thinking time – when ideas come, and possibilities emerge for me to explore and muse over.'

HOBBIES

Peacefulness is derived from deep satisfaction and contentment, and hobbies can offer just such opportunities. People who have hobbies often speak of the absorption they feel and the pleasure they derive from them. You could say they provide a satisfying peacefulness, an inner contentment that allows a person to stick at what they are doing for hours on end, losing track of time. Whether it's crafting wood, creating through the lens of a camera, planting and nurturing plants, painting landscapes, the hobby compels and satisfies, and rewards the hobbyist with a deep creative contentment. Peacefulness.

Case study

Frank Hornby – the inventor of Meccano in 1901 – was a bookkeeper by trade, but during his leisure time was passionately interested in inventing things. Hornby had the idea for Meccano while sitting on a train looking out of the window and seeing a collection of cranes on a construction site. Just think, in a different age, had he avoided daydreaming and spent his time absorbed by a laptop, or texting a friend, he might well have missed that moment of inspiration!

Moments of inspiration and motivation frequently emerge at such times of apparent drifting. There, before our idly staring eyes, lies the solution to a problem, the pointer towards change, the signpost to a new idea. An opportunity is missed when we are constantly occupied. Electronic communication and entertainment platforms, in particular, act like blinkers, averting our eyes and brains from both our inner and outer worlds, stymieing the flow of our thoughts and experiences.

That is not to say that we must place a seeking nose to the window on every train, striving to be inspired, hoping that answers will grab us like some fancy advertisement, presenting a solution in the landscape before our eyes. No, it comes from allowing the body and mind to drift into the enjoyment of the moment. From noticing what is passing by; taking pleasure from the trip itself; witnessing life and landscape in snapshots as we pass.

Mental receptivity

In Malcolm Gladwell's 2005 book *Blink*, he highlights the power of 'thinking without thinking' as a factor in any successful endeavour. He examines the powerful capacity the human mind has to draw instinctively on our experiences and react or respond to situations and problems with effective snap judgements. This is a powerful facility, but it has to be developed. As Goethe rightly said, 'talent develops in solitude, character in the stream of life.' To be instinctive in our thinking and appraising we have to consolidate in silence.

Much of the modern world feeds into our subsconscious mind and makes us think things without being aware that we are being primed in certain ways. Think of the last time you watched a sports car commercial. They didn't just show you the car plonked in front of you on the screen and list all the great things about it. Oh no! There were fast-pulsating images of luxurious steel, leather and chrome, stimulating ambient music, a glorious setting through which the car sped. Your brain waves were very subtly being primed to attach and relate emotional responses to all those images. You now associate luxury, speed, quality, emotion with that car, and probably would like to own it! Or at least like to experience the feelings that all those tempting images conjured up. The technical details of the car seem somewhat superfluous by comparison. Image is a big factor in our fad-ridden and fashion-conscious world.

Developing more awareness and attentiveness is a counter-balance to fast, unconscious thinking. We do have, and need, the capacity for both. Alert, sharp, perceptive, snappy thinking and more considered, slower, more intuitive thinking, too – our brains have the capacity for both. We should not sacrifice one for the other. Neither should we perceive one as superior to the other – by seeing both as essential we avoid the pitfalls of brainwashing and inattentiveness. We combine conscious and unconsious thought in a productive mix.

Focus points
❋ Value the time you have to yourself by noticing your responses.
❋ Make solitude work for your goals rather than against them.
❋ We creak with the weight of complexity – lighten your load.
❋ High expectation frequently means low tolerance. Strike the balance.
❋ Slow thinking frequently leads to wisdom. Ask the tortoise!

Next step

You may have some questions at this point, such as:

✳ The will is there to do things differently and more slowly, but my head says it's impractical – what can I do about that?

✳ I know I am ambitious, so how could solitude get me where I want to be in life?

✳ Don't rest and peacefulness just make you lazy?

✳ How can I sustain peacefulness when life is so 'full-on'?

It isn't until you really start to engage with solitude that you begin to notice your, often unexpected, emergent responses. Sometimes there is resistance. Sometimes it takes time to relax and go with the flow, but always the head and heart begin to connect.

Integrating the two is what we will look at next...

6

Head and Heart

In this chapter you will learn:

▶ *about sustaining peacefulness*
▶ *about integrating your head and heart*
▶ *about making direct choices.*

How do you feel?

Before you begin this chapter, ask yourself the following questions:

1 What do you think you can learn from a simpler life?

2 How might distance help you gain perspective?

3 How do you keep a sense of curiosity and wonder?

4 How much of your time is spent on autopilot?

5 Do you rest well?

Sustaining peacefulness

In every work that he undertook, he did it with all his heart and prospered.

2 Chronicles 31:21 (NIV Bible)

It is one thing experiencing peacefulness in a solitary moment; it is quite another maintaining it, especially when we go back into the fray of everyday living and full functionality. We often hear the phrase 'putting your back into it' in association with work, while 'putting your heart and soul' into something is more likely associated with a passion or hobby. Combining conscious thought and intuitive, instinctive feeling is about integrating the head and the heart in thinking and doing. Making associations between a peaceful contemplative life and an active and engaged one is a challenge. Holding the two together in paradoxical tension is something to attempt when using solitude as part of a successful life.

Here, I believe, we can learn something from monastic life.

In 2005 monks at Worth Abbey in West Sussex, in the UK, gave five ordinary men a 40-day monastic experience within the walls of their community. The men came from all walks of life, and included a retired teacher, a painter and decorator, and a businessman, but together they all experienced a monastic rhythm of living which taught them some profound truths about their lives and inner selves.

A balancing daily rhythm, a routine if you like, of work, study, rest and contemplation (prayer for some), has a grounded stabilizing element to it, allowing the body to respond physically and cognitively. Our physical selves are nourished and respected by variations between work activity and quieter study, reflection or rest, and the mind becomes clearer, more aware, in tune. These are the features of many monastic communities across different faiths.

Frequently, it is thought that *separation* from the everyday world, like the detachment and withdrawal of a monk or nun, is an escape from the reality and challenge of living. Yet it is, as the men at Worth found, the very place for deepening understanding, finding a clearer perspective and setting greater challenges for oneself. Without all the things we hide behind and protect ourselves with – props such as wealth, comfort, status and ephemeral successes – there is no distraction from the self.

Monastic communities make their living by using the collective creative and cognitive gifts and abilities of their members, whether by making pottery or honey, or caring for the sick or educating the young. They see these as vocations to be valued and respected within the context of an integrated, stable and thoroughly grounded life. In seeking happiness and riches we, however, reach out constantly for pleasurable fixes, even if it makes us stressed in the process. True and lasting happiness is more likely found in stability and completeness, from finding contentment in the unification of mind and body. It is the reuniting of the fragmented and fractured life that modern living creates.

Stability is achieved through perseverance, through holding on even under great strain, without weakening or trying to escape. It involves endurance, a virtue we do not often talk about today.
                                    Esther de Waal, *Seeking God*

Case study

When I gave up my burning inner ambition for getting to the top of my career ladder, I relaxed more and enjoyed my life more. I let the reins loosen a little and ended up finding that the things I wanted came to me anyway and now I get far less stressed and frustrated with other people.

Try it now: Make a 'head and heart' list

Make a list of the things you do in a day that are based on head decisions and a separate one of heart decisions. For example: *head* – get to work on time, fill car up with fuel; *heart* – putting a coin in a charity box, buying a pair of new shoes. Which activities are based on feelings and which on the demands of circumstance? Do you have a balance?

Closeness and distance

BEING TOO CLOSE

It is not just about spending time away from others that helps us learn the principles of a quiet heart, but also the giving up of restlessness and striving in order to achieve. We need to acquire stillness within our hearts, so that whatever we are doing, or wherever we are, we can draw upon the strength of silence and stillness to help us, especially in challenging situations. As we gradually learn how to cultivate states of quietness, introspection, retrospection and contemplation, little by little we begin to grow the capacity for more and therefore can more easily transpose them into different situations.

Have you ever been so up close to a situation that you have not been able to see the wood for the trees? You get a general impression, but not the whole picture.

When I am writing directly on to my computer, all I see on the screen is a couple of small paragraphs at the most. My eyes are not able to view the layout, shape and style of the whole document. It isn't until I have printed off a copy that I begin to see some of the blindingly obvious changes I need to make. The difficulty is one of perspective. Close-up or myopic views are useful for some activities, but for me, when I have a whole document, I need to see how the whole thing is looking now and again. It is sometimes frustrating not to see the whole view.

Once you have stepped back from the situation, you are able to gain a broader knowledge of the facts. When you are alone with your thoughts and instincts, you have the freedom to see the fuller picture without obfuscation or distraction. This is a gift, too, of time and breathing space. It allows you to spot the gaps between the trees and see a more detailed and complete picture.

When you are alone, there is more chance of being entirely yourself. There's no pretence or show of courage or confidence, which may mask the situation. You are 'who you are' to yourself, which is a place from which you can honestly see and hear. Away from laptop, tablet, email, phone and TV, you have the space to think and be with yourself and attend to your thoughts only. You are not reacting or responding to anything other than yourself; there's no networking, no running commentary.

There is a distinction to be drawn between trying different actions to achieve a goal and reflecting on these as a possible set of actions before performing them. This latter activity – the planning kind – involves the temporary suspension of overt action and a turning of attention inwards upon mental acts instead.

Margaret Donaldson, *Children's Minds*

GETTING SOME DISTANCE

Distance gives us a wider perspective. It also makes the heart grow fonder, though that's another story!

Have you ever stood at the top of a hill, or travelled on a low-level flight path, or above the clouds, and looked beyond where you are to a distant landscape. Weren't you completely amazed that you were seeing in a very different way? Even the clouds are completely different from the upper side as opposed to the underside. They are pure white, even when they are black underneath.

I once flew in a light aircraft over my own home and was amazed at how very different it looked from the air. Steep slopes looked flat and trees were spaced in patterns I hadn't ever seen or considered before. Reality is different from a distance.

A 'helicopter view' of a situation broadly encompasses and brings into your field of vision things beyond your usual and familiar horizons. This in itself creates a kind of peacefulness.

A sense that things are not exactly as we thought can be liberating, forcing us to think more openly and perceptively.

Time in solitude enables us to gain this valuable treetop view of our life journey, as we are travelling along. When we prioritize to pause and survey the view, it becomes possible to ensure we are not running off in directions we had not originally intended to go, and to gain the benefit of directional signs that keep us on the track we know to be sound and true.

Try it now: Making choices

We need to snap out of autopilot a little more often, particularly when it comes to making decisions. These are harder to make when there is so much confusion, chaos, noise or distraction all around us. To cope, we can easily fall into autopilot mode and do what we always do, or feel pressured to do. We make a snap decision based on little more than habit. In other words, we've made no real decision at all.

Next time you need to make a decision – even about something relatively trivial – try the following technique:

✻ Go to a calm, peaceful place, your special spot in the house, perhaps, or a tranquil corner of your local park.

✻ Clear your mind of every distraction and focus on your decision from close to. What do you 'see'?

✻ Imagine yourself to be up in the sky, looking down at yourself – and the decision you have to make – from high above. Now what do you see. Has the decision simplified itself? Have you gained a new and vigorous perspective?

From rest to success

Restful times give us much more than just rest. J. Warren, in his book *Headtrip* (2007), explores the behaviour of the brain at times when it is in a semi-wakeful state and the opportunity it has for highly productive thinking at these times. He identifies *hypnogogic* and *hypnopompic* experiences as strange states of mental productivity occurring at times of entry into, or exit out of, sleep. The word 'hypnogogic' is derived from the Greek for *hypnos* (sleep) and *agogos* (leading in) while the *pompe* in hypnopompic means 'sending away'. The time between sleep and wakefulness, therefore, is a strange period of odd visions, thoughts, feelings and sensory sensations.

Rest is also a time when the brain engages in consolidation – when it carefully compartmentalizes thoughts and experiences and prepares the body for recovery. This time of restful unconsciousness helps us dim blind ambition, check our motivations, and make sense of the world, as well as rest and regenerate. Sleep restores mind – body and soul. We should not be too swift to skip it!

Remember this: Rest breeds success

Think of the cheetah: It can run at 70 miles per hour, but can sustain that optimum speed only for short bursts. To perform at peak and successfully hunt and prey it must rest in between.

Key idea: Solitude brings true rest

Solitude gives us some of the benefits of sleep while we are awake. Bring to mind the restoring and refreshing feelings you feel when you have had a good walk alone in the open air.

Seeking understanding

Time away from distraction, in solitude, is the place where our heart and head meet and the reality of ourselves is given a chance to rise to the surface. We become more able to stand back and view our situation, with all its predicaments, from a wider perspective while keeping our feet on the ground of personal reality. Life calls to us to be true to ourselves, and not to act solely according to the approval of others.

Peacefulness provides us with a place from which energy, motivation and potential can be drawn in order to reach the potential of the person we truly can be – a place where we are not tossed about by every gust that would blow us off course – the words, ideas and attitudes of others, the vagaries of marketing or the pressures and assumptions of society. In such a place we can truly reconcile head and heart and find our own 'inner monastery'.

Case study

I have a somewhat mentally demanding job with little room for creativity. Gradually, I realized that I needed a channel for a creative part of me. It had been neglected and that neglect had dragged me down. I took up watercolour painting. Eventually I decided to go part-time and do more painting. I now sell these and ironically feel more successful and less chained to a job that seems to take up all of my energy, but not 'require' all of me.

The fulfilment of who we truly are is closely related to the spiritual aspect of our lives, an aspect which is evidently within all of us, but which often is the least invested in. Deliberate reflective solitude brings heart and head together – directing us towards our spiritual, authentic self.

Focus points

* Sustain peacefulness through daily balance.
* Think head and heart.
* Get some distance and perspective when facing challenges and decisions.
* Reawaken childhood wonder and curiosity.
* Snap out of autopilot.

Next step

You may have some questions at this point, such as:

* But how can I stop distractions?
* Are there specific exercises I can do that will help?
* How can I organize time and space for solitude?

To sustain peacefulness and to draw on its benefits, it is important to teach yourself a few exercises to help develop a disciplined approach to integrating solitude in your life. The next chapter will identify some methods and exercises that you can try...

7

Dim Distraction and Refocus Attention

In this chapter you will learn:

▶ *about letting go of perpetual communication*

▶ *about creating peaceful physical and mental space*

▶ *about refocusing attention.*

How do you feel?

Before you begin this chapter, ask yourself the following questions:

1 Do worry and anxiety drive you?

2 Could time alone ever be a possibility for you?

3 Where do you go to give yourself space to think clearly?

4 What do you do to re-energize and recollect yourself?

Nourishment for the soul

We are distracting ourselves into oblivion.

Ronald Rolheiser, *Seeking Spirtuality*

Souls cry out for nourishment from different sources. We wouldn't expect a plant to survive when its basic needs for water, light and warmth are not met. It may just hang on in there and not die, but it won't flourish into a healthy specimen either. It will merely exist. Likewise, the human body and soul will survive without the spiritual nourishment of solitude, but they will never reach their full potential.

Solitude is where the spiritual roadmap is most likely to be revealed. In *Seeking Spirtuality* (Hodder and Stoughton 1998), Rolheiser describes three factors that distract us from developing our full depth of being, and, I believe, a depth of social understanding, engagement and regard for others as well – which most people would recognize as an important part of life even if they have no faith or religion. He cites '(1) Narcissism; (2) Pragmatism; (3) Unbridled restlessness' and explains these as follows:

1 *narcissism* – excessive self-preoccupation;

2 *pragmatism* – excessive focus on work, achievement and the practical concerns of life

3 *unbridled restlessness* – excessive greed for experience.

If we use the metaphor of a garden to represent the life-giving cycle of solitude and peacefulness, we can perhaps see the logic and purpose of these downtimes more clearly. Plants and flowers grow with a single purpose – to pollinate and procreate – yet they exist in collective harmony with other plants and trees. Integral to the natural world is the interdependence of life, growth, beauty and pleasure, bounty and opportunity. It is the same for the integration of silence and solitude in a demanding life lived both alone and with others in creative harmony.

Remember this: Watch and observe

To watch and observe the garden, even a small patch of flowers or vegetables or a window box, is a peaceful occupation in itself. We capture something of the *spirit* of nature.

Solitude and peacefulness are, however, the very factors that many avoid today, and certainly popular culture would have us steer well and truly clear of them. We are encouraged to be connected with the world all the time through perpetual social and virtual networking, phone and Internet connections, plus a myriad of other channels.

In solitude and silence, the features of our personality, motivations and mindfulness are laid open and heard. It is where we find the *spirit* of who we are; our 'signature', if you like. Here we reconcile ourselves to ourselves. It becomes the reference point from which outside communication with others is made more real and honest, enhanced by the knowledge of our guiding personal principles exposed in solitude.

Many who seek silence or solitude today do so simply to take a break from the 'rat race' – rather than seeking to make more radical changes. There is nothing wrong with this as such, but, if it is also viewed as an opportunity for growth, then far more rewards can be realized. The risk is that the pursuit of silence can become a self-indulgence – motivated merely by the craving to do less or simply chill out, rather than as a genuine move towards balance. It misses the opportunity to plumb the depths of silence and solitude as a reservoir for purposeful living. A well of knowledge and understanding awaits the intrepid explorer. Solitude is the very place where the person you uniquely are is created and transformed.

Letting go of perpetual communication

Our obsession with perpetual communication is not only on occasions rude – we've all been behind that person in the supermarket queue who takes the phone call in the middle of being served by the assistant! – it also impedes the quality of human interaction. We are distracted by the need to react and respond to texts, emails and phone calls, to engage in social networking and to surf the Internet throughout the day. Some kind of attention deficit disorder seems to be becoming more and more prevalent among adults, who refuse to be selective about their availability for communication beyond their immediate environment, rarely fully attending to those in their actual company.

Try it now: Disconnect to reconnect

Re-engage. Regain some freedom and reconnect with the people around you and your environment. Put the phone away in the evening, or do not take it with you on every trip out. Resist the compulsion to look everything up throughout the day and evening. Resist, too, the compulsion to be in contact with loved ones, friends, acquaintances throughout the day and evening. You may find you:

* feel like you have more time
* get more done
* are not hopping from activity to activity, or place to place, so much
* can concentrate better
* notice more around you
* have less eyestrain
* are more physically active
* are more relaxed
* are less tense
* are more peaceful...

Case study

On walks I no longer take my mobile phone with me. When I first did it, it felt very strange; I felt naked without it. But it didn't take long before I realized just how much I needed this kind of detachment – to be unreachable. Constant connection drains my capacity for thought and pulls my mind into places and concerns beyond where I am at the time. It unhinges me and does not let me ground myself. It is like a constantly binding leash that allows me only a short rein before hauling me in again.

Reinforce peacefulness

In the following section (and in Appendix 2) you will find some practical exercises that will help you to reinforce peacefulness. Try to take small opportunities throughout every day to be less distracted and peaceful no matter what you are doing. If you are feeling tense or frustrated, use some of the following exercises to help deal with them.

Try implementing one of the following for a week and then introduce others as you master each:

▶ **Take ten** Use this when you are angry, frustrated, annoyed or stressed. Make a conscious decision to *stop*. Sit or stand still with your eyes closed if possible. Breathe in and out slowly as you count to ten in your head. This gives you a short mental space to catch your thoughts and avoid the risk of reacting out of anger or frustration.

▶ **Breathing break** Sit or stand comfortably wherever you are. Drop the tension in your shoulders, back, neck and so on. Lift your diaphragm and take a long, slow breath in for the count of five. Hold your breath for the count of five, then breathe out slowly for the count of five, releasing tension as you do so. *Repeat three times.* You will begin to feel more relaxed and refreshed from the greater amount of oxygen in your lungs and feel more energized because of the deeper breathing. We tend to breathe very shallowly when we are busy, stressed or occupied, especially when slumped in a chair or in front of a computer.

▶ **Stimulating stretch** Wherever you are, get into the habit of taking a few seconds to elongate and stretch out your neck, limbs and torso and rotate the arms in sweeping, windmill-like movements. This revives and invigorates stressed parts of your body. You will feel more invigorated if this exercise is carried out both before and after a long period of sitting or standing. It helps with concentration and refreshes cognitive function.

▶ **Go for a walk** This is crucial if you do a sedentary job. Walking is a good way to reduce stress, renew energy and provide fresh air and exercise to invigorate the mind and body. It also provides space for you to clear your head of mental pressures and encourages better rest and sleep. Take a short ten-minute walk during working days during lunch or coffee breaks. Map yourself a route, preferably circular, and keep up a medium-paced rhythm to the walk. Carried out in solitude, the psychomotor movement helps you reflect, unwind and refresh. This is good to practise at the beginning and end of the day, too, if you can manage it. Try to do short bursts of walking, not too quickly, but deliberately and mindfully.

▶ **Admire a view** If you drive long distances for work, make sure you take a few minutes to stop and admire a view. This helps with concentration and keeps tiredness at bay, but you can also use it as an awareness raiser and 'distraction dimmer', too. You will become more aware and appreciative of the passing surroundings and environment. If you also do one of the exercises above at the same time, it will recharge the batteries as well.

▶ **Relaxed repose** Depending on the kind of work and life pace you live at, try to do a relaxation exercise every day or, at the very least, a couple of times a week. There are good CDs and DVDs available to help you with this, but you can implement something for yourself, too. Put on some fairly quiet relaxing music, preferably with no distracting lyrics. Take up a comfortable position in a warm and open space in your home. Lie on your back on the floor with a blanket under you. Think of one word – for example, 'peace', 'air' or 'breath' – and repeat it slowly as you breathe gently in and out. Do the 'breathing break' exercise as above – in and out for five counts each – as you say your one word. Then tense and gently release each set of muscles *in turn* from your face and head down through your shoulders, arms, stomach, back and buttocks, to your legs and toes, until you feel relaxed. Be aware of both your breathing and your word. Complete with a minute of total stillness before gently coming to a sitting position. This exercise can also be done fairly effectively in a comfortable chair. You should feel a reduction of tension and a relaxation of your mind as you sink into the experience.

▶ **Contemplative corner** At either, the beginning, middle or end of each day, take yourself to a corner of a room, or better still a garden or park, where you can be alone for five to ten minutes. If at home, light a candle. If at work, go to a quiet room or outside. Sit, or stand, in total silence. Concentrate on one thing before you. If at home, look at the silent flickering of the candle flame. If in a garden, study the silent beauty of a flower, plant or insect. In the park, stand beneath a tree and contemplate its silent strength, height and age. Just be in the moment... in a contemplative corner of your day.

Creating a haven of peacefulness

We've heard it many times before but less really is more!

Whether it be the clutter of physical possessions, the clutter of activity and involvement, or simply a question of the million and one thoughts that beset our waking lives, it is important to learn to clear the decks and find space to breath. It's true: The mind and body become more efficient with less. Keeping things simple and uncluttered facilitates clearer thinking and more efficient working.

Think of the last time you tried to fix the car, bake a cake, or arrange a holiday when there was mess or confusion before you started. I am sure the more muddle there was in the garage or kitchen, or the more choices you had about what to do and where to go, the harder the job was to carry through.

You will have heard this message many, many times, in different places and in different ways, not least in popular magazines. Decluttering purges the mind and spirit. At the same time, however, we are still persuaded through advertising to keep buying more things and to have more experiences. We simply add different clutter even as we are throwing the old clutter away.

It seems like an unbreakable cycle, but by trying to eliminate the muddles, the superfluous and excess of choices, you can make steps along the pathway to a little more peacefulness of mind, not to mention fewer responsibilities, because there is less to take care of or process. Do not be tempted to replace it all with other things instead, though!

Try it now: Find an oasis of peacefulness

Prioritize time, just 15 or 20 minutes, in your working day to seek out a place in which to be alone. It may be a walk alone to a park near your office, or a corner of your garden at home. If you're lucky enough to have a garden or small rest area at your place of work, take your sandwiches and sit alone for a while. For some, a church building is a still and quiet space to reflect or pray. Don't use this time to catch up on your text messages, socialize with others, catch up on chores, but fill it with... nothing. Detach yourself from all external communication for just a few short minutes each day and you will reap rich rewards.

A disciplined approach to decluttering is by far the best solution. Discipline means hard work, I hear you say. Actually, it is more about *mindful* work. Thinking back to the roots of why you want to *have* something, or *do* a particular thing, will enable you to decide whether it really is important or not. Your motivation for having it and doing it is by far the best indicator of whether you really need it or not. Assess this against the values you have about life, to help you decide what to stick to and what to drop.

WHERE'S BEST?

Where do you make space for yourself? Do you have a place or places you can go to be alone for a while? Being in close proximity to others is naturally rewarding and sociable, but if you want to be quiet and peaceful, uninterrupted for a while, where do you go? If you have nowhere particular, think about how you can create that special place.

Creating a small space every day to be alone can pay dividends with inner peacefulness. It could be a small area of your home; a sitting place at work away from others works well. Some offices and places of work have designated rest areas, though many are social gathering places – for example the coffee lounge, the canteen and so on.

Best of all, though – if at all possible – is a space in your garden – tranquil, green and secluded. This has been my solution and it has transformed my life so deeply that, to spread my message, I make my space in my garden available once a month for people to come along and take time out alone in quiet solitude. I am not alone in my choice.

The UK-founded Quiet Garden Movement (quietgarden.org) has over the last 20 years grown into an international network of gardens where people can do this very thing. Increasingly, employers, too, are recognizing the need for staff to take time to relax and recover in more peaceful surroundings, so some are building small courtyard garden areas, or a comfortable seating space where gentle music plays. If you are lucky enough to have one of these in your place of work, make sure that work talk or informal meetings do not spill into these areas; they should be carefully managed in order to avoid such habits taking hold.

Case study

I wanted a place in the house to sit and think; a place to myself where I could stop with a cup of tea and rest, away from the TV. Yet every time I cleared a spot I'd leave books and magazines there and little by little things would crowd in on me. I had to break the habit of leaving things around and not take anything with me into my quiet space.

Calming anxiety

The drip, drip, drip of anxiety is instilled into us from a very young age. Think about the following modern fears that from early on are inculcated into children:

▶ *Stranger danger* – the world beyond home is a dangerous place. Keep away from it!

▶ *The sun* – is dangerous to our health and will cause harm. Stay out of it!

▶ *Roads* – are dangerous, fast and busy. You can't walk to school!

▶ *Food* – can cause health problems. Avoid them!

One day I found one of my sons, aged eight, reading food labels after a lesson at primary school on healthy eating. He said we should no longer be eating yoghurt, milk or cheese because they all had more than 5 per cent fat. These have been staple foods for centuries, but he had been scared into believing they were harmful. Education that instils this level of concern, fear and anxiety is probably as harmful to health as a few extra percentage points of fat in our food. Education should be more positive in its approach.

Like the propaganda fed to us by 'distress advertising', we reach a point where we can no longer make proper sense of the world, or of what is necessary and appropriate for *us*. Keep yourself informed, yes, but do not make yourself over-anxious with thoughts that eat away at your peacefulness. Anxiety reduces energy and resilience.

Case study

As I started to clear away the mental clutter of negative things that I naturally seemed to hoard in my mind – thoughts like 'You are always late', 'You never finish things' and so on – I began to feel a sense of clarity about what I should let go of and what was part of my real identity. I began to see that actually all these thoughts were a misrepresentation. Sometimes I am late, but *mostly* I am on time. Sometimes I don't finish things, but *mostly* I do. Time reflecting on this and journaling it helped me grasp a more realistic appreciation of who I am.

The well of yourself

In business management and commerce we are familiar with the word 'resourcing', meaning the supply of people, skills, facilities and money. 'Resources' are the organization's working capital in terms of human, financial, property and knowledge assets. Take a look at yourself and you will see that you are similarly resourced with talents and capabilities that enable you to build capital assets of experience, skills, knowledge and understanding.

Solitude enables you to go back to the *source* of who you are – a well, if you like, from which you draw refreshment from deep within the centre of the person that is you. Yes, when you dip your metaphorical bucket deep into the well of your inner self you risk finding a little muck and mould as well as clean and clear refreshing water. Alone, we sit with the whole of ourselves, the good and the not so good. But how is it possible to be authentic, true and genuine, if you persist in hiding the rubbish?

Within the crowd of people – family, friends, colleagues – that surrounds you, you are a reflection of yourself. You reflect to others what is on the inside of you. Time alone helps you see what really should come to the surface. In times of aloneness, when you have only yourself to 'talk' to, you gain a oneness with your inner self.

Remember this: Review your resources

Businesses and organizations regularly monitor and review their resources to ensure peak performance and maximum efficiency, and take on new resources where there may be gaps. Similarly, we should review and realign our own personal resources. At a personal level, a review like this is more a process of inner reflection, 're-viewing' your interior strengths, skills and capability.

Look at the word 'resource' slightly differently. Try to understand it from a slightly different perspective and it takes on a more valuable meaning. *Re-source* – to source again;

to go back to the source; to refresh and replenish. By going back to the well of the self during moments of peacefulness, you can not only renew your energy but also draw upon hidden strengths and capabilities that may have long been hidden from your view.

Try it now: Be mindful

Try the following ideas to make yourself more mindful of your surroundings, what's going on right now:

* Next time you are in the corridor at work, on the bus, train or at the supermarket, try being more attentive to what is going on around you.
* Next time you are alone at home, sit at the window awhile and just watch.
* Next time you are out walking, don't talk but just take in your surroundings.

The more you practise this kind of attentiveness, the more you will find that you gain an accurate perspective on what is going on around you. You will begin to focus better and become more thorough and careful when you need to take action. This brings with it a more peaceful sense of balance as you see the fruits of *responding* rather than merely reacting.

Focus points

* Try and let go of the need for perpetual communication – disconnect from 'machine-assisted' living a little more.
* Take the opportunity for short, restful, de-stressing practical exercises throughout the day and week.
* Clear away clutter – in mind and environment.
* Create less distress and anxiety and resource yourself.

Next step

You may have some questions at this point, such as:

✳ I want to live with more awareness of peacefulness, but am not sure what else I can do to do so?

✳ How can I give myself more valuable solitary time?

✳ What do I need to do to build on my initial steps into solitude?

Remind yourself that you make more sustainable progress when you break a challenge down into small steps. It builds up your confidence to take on the next stage if you keep each step simple. Consider it a pathway into peacefulness...

8

Pathways to Peacefulness

In the chapter you will learn:

- ► *about the pathways to peacefulness*
- ► *about making a retreat*
- ► *about what to take with you into solitude*
- ► *transferring the experience of solitude into everyday life.*

Self-assessment

Before you begin this chapter, ask yourself the following questions:

1 How do you make yourself peaceful?

2 What proportion of your time is spent in silence?

3 Could you make a solitary retreat?

4 How might your life benefit from having short time-out experiences?

5 Does the environment you work or live in make you peaceful?

One of the aspects of dependency is that it is unconcerned with spiritual growth. Dependent people are interested in their own nourishment, but no more; they desire filling, they desire to be happy; they don't desire to grow, nor are they willing to tolerate the unhappiness, the loneliness and suffering involved in growth.

M. Scott Peck, *The Road Less Travelled*

Solitude and peacefulness not only provide a healthy counter-balance to our physically and mentally demanding lives, they are frequently bearers of wisdom, too. Taking time to reflect, recharge and refocus attention is a revealing and enhancing mental experience. The growth of wisdom comes through the silence. We miss out on the opportunity if we don't invest time and space. It may be painful to search oneself honestly, to reflect with a degree of humility on one's comings and goings, but the age-old adage that 'pain is gain' does indeed ring true in this case. We grow and develop through silence as well as through full-on action.

Self-discovery, or, as I prefer to call it, self-creativity, is born of honest scrutiny and preparedness for change. Learning to be by oneself, with oneself, is sometimes uncomfortable, but it is a pathway to insight and wisdom. Wisdom enables us to discern the right pathways for our lives. Routes that fit who and how we are in our uniqueness. There we can shed the burden of external expectations and begin to be true to ourselves first. Then we are ready to face the world squarely.

Retreat

The word 'retreat' suggests a running away from something, a turning tail and scarpering. I have a much more positive take on it. Just as the tide ebbs (withdraws) and flows (returns), so, too, should a healthy and balanced life, physically and mentally – whatever our spiritual or religious beliefs. We get to know our individual tolerances over time. Reflecting in solitude can help us identify the personal motivations that cause us to lose our balance and slip into unhealthy ways.

Holidays are meant to enable us to have a break from the usual routine and regain our rebalance. It's time spent away from work or home, during which we refresh and restore ourselves and recuperate. But, frequently, holidays are full of demands and stresses in themselves these days. We travel long distances, make highly complicated travel plans, and perhaps even take *too many* holidays through the year. Hampered by airport security and transport delays, among many other things, we merely end up increasing the load, not lightening it. There was tongue-in-cheek irony in the film *Home Alone*. The distinct possibility that you might forget a child in the hectic rush to get you and the family to a plane on time demonstrates what pressures a holiday can create.

In reality, though, we do not have to travel far or have permanent sunshine and out-and-out luxury to have the kind of break that restores balance. A short break, even just an hour or two, half a day, or a whole day, from home and work, if it contains the right conditions for time out from stress and pressure, is restoring. We have to focus our attention on recovery, not on 'pleasure fixes', which is what holidays have largely become.

If you have never retreated alone before, it will probably feel a little alien, so it is best to begin by taking brief times away at first.

GET A SHED!

In traditional Russia, the word *poustinia* was used for a small and simple cabin out in the woods. These were sparsely furnished, with just somewhere to lie or sit down, with water, blanket and not much else. People would visit these huts on their wanderings and spend a day, or more, living simply there. If prayer was important to them, they would also pray for the community nearby, and sometimes they would even contribute manual labour in between the bouts of solitude.

Of course, you don't need to visit Russia to get your own *poustinia* experience – your retreat to nature could simply be the shed at the bottom of the garden. Hang out there for an hour or two, without doing anything but enjoying the pleasure of your own company. You might like to listen to some soft instrumental music or sip a long soft drink. It will be more relaxing if you can make the shed simple and free of clutter as possible – perhaps with just a cosy old armchair and a blanket and cushion.

You could, of course, take a cottage or caravan somewhere fairly remote for a weekend. Engage only simple activities – you could take along some art materials, a notepad for writing, soft music and so on. The point is to be alone without distractions from the outside world, so definitely don't take things like a mobile phone or laptop. This is an occasion when the lack of a signal is a good thing!

Case study

The small shed in my garden is where I go to be alone. It has very little in it, which is precisely its appeal; I can leave all that I usually have around me back at the house. I have a chair in there, a small table and a big mug for my coffee. From the window I can see a small fruit tree where I watch all kinds of visiting birds. It takes me back to making a den when I was a child. It's a simple place, hidden from view, where the imagination can flow!

Retreat is particularly special for those with family commitments – it is a wonderful feeling to get up in the morning with only yourself to think about, moving into the day at your own pace, without a timetable dictated by other people's needs, schedules, deadlines and expectations. It is very liberating – like a breath of fresh air.

Releasing ourselves from our commitments – even for a short while – is not always easy to achieve, but when it is possible it can be a very valuable experience.

Figure 8.1 A peaceful place to reflect and be. Note how few things there are in my 'shed' – a desk and chair, a candle and writing equipment. Everything you need for an hour's solitude, and nothing more.

LONGER RETREATS

Of course, if a longer retreat is feasible, take the opportunity. I have been practising this for more than seven years now, annually taking myself to an isolated location, where I am alone for a whole working week. I take my writing with me and nothing else. It focuses and refreshes me, even though I am working. It is never *very* far away; this is deliberate – I do not want to add the burden of a long journey. I like to slip away easily and simply, taking very little with me. One retreat was just 25 minutes from home, but it still felt like worlds away.

These seven years have been a voyage of great personal discovery for me, though one not without its difficulties and challenges. One of the most significant discoveries has been the value I place on my family and community being heightened by the experience. Yes, absence really does make the heart feel fonder. When we are alone for extended periods of time, our pleasure in, and our desire for, the company of our family, friends and neighbours is sharpened, while at the same time it gives us the space we need to be ourselves for a while. Of course, such extended retreats require thoughtful preparation, in order to both cater for one's own needs and to assure the wellbeing of your family that you are leaving for a while. It is to the tricky subject of preparation that I turn to next.

Case study: A week in solitude

Born into a large family, there was never really any peaceful time. We were always talking, doing and going places. I was conditioned into restlessness. Rarely could I experience being alone with my true self, though, I admit, I did daydream often! Later, too, with husband and three sons to care for and nurture, time for silence and solitude was limited.

As children turned to teenagers, glimmers of solitude beckoned but it felt alien. It was not until after turning forty, when the children were growing into adulthood, that I decided it was time to take a solitary retreat. It would be the first protracted time alone in my entire life! I would go alone taking just my writing and a few books. I would be travelling light, with simple food requiring no cooking, relaxed clothing and just a few toiletries. With only my needs to think about, preparation was minimal. Again alien territory!

Released from the chains of distraction and demands, I motored along in silence, feeling a mixture of both anticipation and fear – anticipation of the pleasures I had planned for and fear that perhaps after all I would not cope and would feel lonely.

Arriving at the tiny cottage in the countryside where I would stay for one week, totally alone and with no technological connections to the 'outside world', I began to unpack. Alertness and sensitivity to the newness of the environment came upon me. It took time to settle my mind, but I allowed myself to go with this transitional restlessness.

When I awoke the next morning, this new environment had somehow become more familiar. My restlessness began to dwindle. As I ate my simple breakfast, with no radio, television, or family to distract me, I suddenly became aware of the food and what it meant to my body that day. I was paying attention to the importance of nourishment to the body and soul.

Gathering my books, laptop and writing materials, I chose a place within the quaint, old cottage to settle for my working day. Oh, how the silence felt loud! I felt a strange mixture of relief and anxiety. Was I up to being totally alone for a whole day? A whole week? Working in complete aloneness! I put on a CD of pleasant, instrumental music – no words to stir my memories or distract my thoughts – just music. This seemed to quieten my doubts a little.

I began to write. Body and mind worked comfortably together for about an hour, before I became restless again. I needed to move. I stood and stretched. I wandered and paused by a window. The scene seemed to speak silent words to me. I realized that casting off my addiction to perpetual connectivity – the stimulations of people, Internet, phone and activity – was going to take time. Directing my attention towards what was about me in the here and now, I knew, would help. Over the minutes, as I let myself relax, I found myself becoming increasingly aware of and engaged with my environment and the world beyond disappeared. Like an uncurling leaf, I felt as if I were stretching outwards and opening up. I settled back to work again.

I discovered the rhythm of my coming days: the gentle pattern of movement, lyric-less music, simple food, short bursts of work and reflection sustained me. As I went with this rhythm, new ideas came flooding in, inspiring and energizing me. Each day brought a deeper creativity and a heightened awareness and respect for the life balance I was discovering. I was learning more about myself. I found that there were 'natural' times in the day when I felt more like working and others when I just wanted to sit and reflect. Over time my creative energy welled up and blossomed in my work.

Halfway through the week a longing for a little company began to rear up, but I set it aside and instead worked through my fear of aloneness. I did not allow myself to wallow in dissatisfaction and applied myself to some sketching or reading.

When I finally returned to my home and family, I felt more whole and complete for having had the experience of solitude, I felt deeper gratitude for what my life had given me, and was able to engage more richly with those around me. I felt that I understood so much more about myself and what lies hidden within all of us.

Above all, I had come to recognize that the need for solitary time as an integral part of my life.

(You will find a whole 'menu' of retreats for you to try in Appendix 1.)

PREPARATION

The most difficult challenge for many is the transition from busyness to quietness. It is not just a question of leaping into the car and driving into the blue yonder. You must prepare carefully, with thought given to where you will go, what you will take with you, what you will leave behind and what you might occupy yourself with while there. Much of this is naturally personal choice, but I include here a checklist of things that I believe deserve attention and which will maximize the benefits you will gain from your peaceful time:

▶ **Choose the right location.** It doesn't have to be very far from your home, but a quiet spot; a place with a view might help.

▶ **Take time and thought when packing.** What you pack will depend largely on what you will do once you are there, but I recommend taking nothing except the things you need for walking (a stout pair of shoes), for your meals (keep it simple!) and for a hobby such as painting – remember it is not meant to be a holiday filled with activity!

▶ **Remember, NO electronic gadgets.** The object of the exercise is to disconnect for a time, so gadgets should on no account be taken. I am usually in an area where it is not possible to get a signal anyway. Take a phone *if you must*, but discipline yourself not to use it to talk to people every day.

▶ **Make a list of resources.** Take things with you that help you relax. I always take a large scented candle to burn, soft instrumental music, books, art materials, writing equipment.

▶ **Leave once the family are at school/work.** My family are now grown, so what to do with the children is not an issue for me. Putting the right care arrangements in place for younger children is, of course, very important. It helps to leave, though, once everyone has left the house and you can make your departure with a clear head and without feeling overly emotional.

▶ **Make the journey part of the experience.** Plan the route carefully and take your time getting there. You will notice a growing sense of lightness as the miles pass.

Try it now: Make a pamper hamper

Put together a box of objects and provisions that help you become peaceful. This is something I developed about 12 years ago, when I was planning and preparing my own time-out experiences. What you put in your box will to some extent be different for each individual, but some things will be common to most people. For instance:

* soft music
* scented candles
* relaxation/meditation CD and player
* essential oil burner
* notebook and pencil
* relaxation exercises.

You know what creates a peaceful environment for you, so spend a little time thoughtfully putting together a box of resources to be taken with you to places of solitude, either on retreat or kept in a specially set-aside peaceful space at home. You will more regularly use it if it is always ready to go. When out and about, gather odd items to add to the collection, interchanging things if necessary. For example, shells, pebbles, driftwood collected on a previous retreat are evocative things to have around you and engender a sense of place and peace.

Figure 8.2 My pamper hamper...

Make some provision for recording your thoughts, responses and general ruminations while you are on retreat. This gives you a record for the future and useful insight into yourself. This could be a simple diary, of course, but better still would be an audio or video record. These are often better at giving the unvarnished version of your experience of solitude – the pleasures *and* challenges and what you discover about yourself and your values.

Taking steps to integrate retreat into your lifestyle may not be easy. It is much more challenging than simply grabbing a few quiet moments by yourself now and then. It takes careful and thoughtful planning, but the rewards will be rich indeed.

Let's now turn to another path to peacefulness – recreation.

Recreation

I think it is sometimes helpful to break familiar words into component parts, as it helps to provide a slightly different perspective and understanding. Take the word 'recreation', which we are used to associating with leisure, cultural or social pursuits such as taking part in sports, going to the cinema, or socializing with friends and family. Look at the word again: when split, *re-creation* could more meaningfully suggest what this time is meant to do for us – the 're' is evocative of a return to a previous condition, while 'create' means 'cause to come into existence'. So, for me, recreation has connotations of rediscovering one's original self or being.

Do we know our previous condition? Do we have enough change of pace and state to know the difference between our current and previous conditions? When time is consumed by activity, do we ever have an opportunity to 'return to our previous condition', and cause it to come back into existence? Do you know who you are, what state is your best and most nourishing place?

Remember this: The true meaning of recreation

Recreation is not just about fun, but a chance to re-create who you are through a change of activity and pace.

The *Collins Dictionary* defines 'recreation' as 'refreshment of health or spirits by relaxation and enjoyment'. I believe that many of us today focus more on the enjoyment end of the scale – i.e. the fun and the pleasure – than on what is genuinely refreshing and *re-creating* activity. Recreation time should make us anew and give us pleasure in the process. It should also help us recover and return to ourselves, after the demands of physical and mental application imposed upon us by work and modern life.

Try it now: Blue yonder days

When my children were young we had what we called 'blue yonder days'. These usually involved me taking them off with a picnic on a mystery tour. I did not plan for any particular activities – the idea was for us to feel as free and unhampered as possible. To this day, my children still remember the motivating freshness and joy of those days.

To maintain a powerful pulse in our lives, we must learn how to rhythmically spend and renew energy.

Jim Loehr and Tony Schwartz,
The Power of Full Engagement

Environment and 'atmosphere'

As with any learning or growing environment, it is important to try and create conditions that will maximize chances of success. Certain environments speak loudly to us, either for good or bad. Peacefulness may not be acquired only in seemingly perfect harmonious places, but in what at first sight seem unappealing or even 'troubled' spaces, too. It is ultimately your *attitude* and response to that environment that will determine what you feel. It is possible to transcend a troubled environment and remain peaceful, though this takes time and effort to learn and practise.

Key idea: Simplicity

Whether it's a corner of a room, a shed, or a cottage by the sea, an environment must reflect simplicity. At times when you are not in such a place, you can recall to mind the image and feeling of this quiet, peaceful place to help you.

Remember, too, that what we need from an environment will not necessarily be the same for all people. What brings a sense of peacefulness to you may be similar, but with a few subtle differences, to the next person. A decluttered space, a shiny new and inspiring one, or a space full of interesting books or artworks, all speak differently to different people. Find the space that fits *you* – your character, your interests and your personality, all play a part in finding the right space. Start by asking yourself: In what type of environment am I most likely to feel a sense of peace?

Remember this: Tastes differ

The factors that foster peacefulness and enable enjoyment of solitude will not be the same for everyone.

Common physical factors may, however, be:

► a comfortable chair

► a view

► inspiring photos/pictures/objects

► lack of clutter

► natural daylight

► no television or radio etc.

► gentle music.

These things may be found in a small corner of a room, a garden shed, almost anywhere. Again, it is important to sharpen your awareness and begin to recognize what works for you.

Try it now: Find that special place

Try taking a walk around your home and 'sensing' the areas and spaces you appreciate most. It may be the conservatory, or a corner of the living room, or a little attic room. Think about what makes it seem so peaceful and appealing to you, and ask yourself how these qualities might be accentuated and maintained.

Case study

Whenever I have moved to a new home, I have found an almost gravitational pull towards a certain room or area in a room. Almost always this has become the space that makes me feel peaceful, even if I am active there, such as in a dining room or study. I set about accentuating the peaceful qualities of the spot, adding a comfortable chair and a number of carefully chosen things that evoke tranquillity and happiness for me. Getting that peaceful place is partly the result of happenstance and partly your own creation.

Environmental conditions are important, but in addition places have that almost indefinable extra that we call 'atmosphere'. Some places meet all the common criteria – light, warmth, simplicity, a beautiful view – yet just have something about them we find incongruent or disturbing, making it hard for us to settle there and find peace. Trust your instincts – transforming that space, whatever you do to change it and make it your own, may well be impossible.

Case study

I once took a solitary retreat to a small cottage where later I learned there had been some real sadness between the people who had once lived there. Though the place was carefully filled with useful and beautiful things, in all the right spaces, I was unsettled and felt a deep absence of peacefulness.

Work

Work is an interesting and tremendously exciting learning tool when undertaken voluntarily and in ways that do not cripple the spirit.

William S. Coperthwaite, *A Handmade Life*

So far we have largely looked at peacefulness as an antidote to work – almost as its opposite – but work itself can be a source of peacefulness, especially work that engages the mind, hands and body and which is holistically satisfying and enjoyable. It is only when work becomes just a means to an end that it loses its pleasure for us and becomes one-dimensional, eventually repressing any chance for creative and spiritual engagement. Then comes stress!

Work that engages and helps you grow will satisfy and endure. Here people who are prepared not to follow the expected norms of society – to get a qualification, find employment with a good firm, climb the promotion ladder, and so forth – have the advantage. For those who integrate physical work with mental activity and creative or caring roles, there are larger rewards than simply money and mental challenge. Work becomes a true vocational calling, not a professional label that you are eager to shed at retirement.

The driving forces of mass education, consumerism, globalization and wealth creation have helped to dehumanize work, turning workers into little more than thinking machines. In this environment physical, social, caring or craft-based careers have, for some time now, been viewed as 'lesser' vocations and have attracted commensurately reduced salaries.

But there are green shoots of change. Increasingly, people are choosing other ways to earn their living. Furniture-making, creative writing, making fine music, establishing charities and developing organizations that offer help and support in the world are becoming recognized as more rewarding and enriching than the dehumanizing work of the so-called 'professions' – accountancy, law, finance, etc. The tide is turning towards a greater reverence for creative, caring and craft-based skills and abilities, and it is precisely this type of work that breeds peacefulness.

Whatever we apply ourselves to – whatever our craft – we must seek engagement and fulfilment and find the true meaning, value and purpose of what we do, and why we do it. It will then begin to make us feel whole and integrated, rather than driven and fragmented.

In his book *A Handmade Life*, William Coperthwaite, an American teacher, builder, designer and writer, speaks of the people who have influenced him in his working life. These were people who combined together 'sensitivity, intellectual acuity, work with their hands' and 'dedication to a better society'. He describes his ideal work as:

- being physically and intellectually challenging
- encouraging creative thinking
- advancing the cause of a better world
- providing for basic needs.

Wise words indeed!

Remember this: Work needn't be drudgery

We don't have to be wage slaves. We can have a vocation that provides enormous pleasure and satisfaction, if we look for a purpose in what we do.

Work really can bring a sense of peacefulness when meaningfulness and purpose are combined with values that focus on (self and societal) *enrichment* rather than getting rich quick. After all, do we want to get to the end of life and say, 'Look at all I have accrued that I now must leave behind'? Or do we want to be able to say: 'That was one heck of a journey – it gave me satisfaction, pleasure, challenge and opportunities to create, to change the world and to give to others. I'm ready to leave!'?

Life balance

The final path to peacefulness I want to look at in this chapter is what I call 'life balance' – by which I mean the balance between different types of activity you are involved in throughout the day. Let's start with a simple exercise that will elucidate this concept further.

Try it now: Assess your own life balance

* Consider your average kind of day.
* Now write down all the things you do during that day and place them under three headings according to their predominant character:
    1 cognitive
    2 physical
    3 free flow.
For example, working at your computer in the office is *cognitive*. Running to the train station is *physical*. Sitting listening to music is *free flow*.
* What do you notice?

When one area is consistently under- or over-represented compared to others areas, your wellbeing will very likely suffer in the long run. Too much cognitive activity, for example, may make you feel tired, irritable, restless; too much free-flowing activity will make you feel as if your life lacks structure and purpose. Establishing equilibrium between these three core areas is a simple and accessible way to begin to develop a thoughtful approach to maintaining wellbeing. Sufficient balance between the areas increases personal efficiency and productivity, with optimized chances for greater creativity.

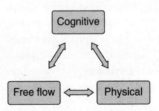

Focus points

* A solitary retreat can be waiting just at the end of the garden.
* A luxurious holiday home in the sun is not essential for a solitary retreat and may be even counterproductive – think simplicity.
* Re-creating is returning to a previous condition. Give yourself the opportunity to re-create!
* Balance your life between physical, cognitive and free-flowing activities.

Next step

You may have some questions at this point, such as:

✳ What type of retreat is best for me to try?
✳ How should I record my retreat experiences?
✳ Are there things I can do, other materials available, to help me direct my retreat time?

It is popular to use a personal life coach these days – someone who can help you balance life's demands and challenges. It can be an expensive luxury, though. So, why not create your own virtual coach by using some simple exercises you can implement during retreat times. You can find these in Appendix 2 at the end of this book.

In the following chapter we are going to look at how you can integrate peacefulness into your life journey...

9

Signposts and Navigation

In this chapter you will learn:

▶ *about using peacefulness in your personal story*

▶ *about the signposts and signals that point towards peacefulness*

▶ *how to develop the 'attitude of gratitude'.*

How do you feel?

Before you begin this chapter, ask yourself the following questions:

1 How do you recognize your need for peacefulness?

2 Do you stop to identify your life direction and pathways?

3 How do you feed your mind and body?

4 How do you note and record gratitude in your life?

5 Would you like to pay more attention to your life as you live it?

Using peacefulness in your personal story

TELLING YOUR STORY

Solitude is a part of everyone's story. Sometimes it is chosen, but sometimes it is forced upon us, through bereavement or other specific circumstances. Finding yourself suddenly alone is in many ways a dreadful prospect, especially if there has been a long preceding period of companionship. Loss and solitude are painful prospects at such a time. Nonetheless, such unchosen solitude can also become a pointer towards a new way of being and doing. It can cause us to review and reassess how one spends personal time and lead us towards a new life.

Case study

Since my husband died a few years ago, though I miss him very much, I have decided to focus on being productive with my time rather than to focus on my loss. I now do creative things like watercolour painting and writing, and now I do a bit of travelling. It has helped me see an extra part of myself beyond who I was in marriage.

In Jung's prologue to his autobiography he expresses the difficulty he had in writing it because when we reflect upon our life there are none of the usual parameters of set standards or objective foundations from which to judge ourselves. In certain ways we can categorize ourselves against other things, and individual beings, but we are, after all, unique, with a unique story to tell. Generalizations and averaging out of the diversity of human life experience is not possible, or desirable; our life story is a one-off and only we have experienced it.

Noticing the features and factors that have contributed towards our life experience can give us valuable insights. Reflecting on our past, on the patterns and the story arc we find there, is helpful in providing useful directional signposts and waymarks. It helps us to consolidate before we move onward to the next chapter of our life. Of course, we could just move on, headlong and reckless, but such a laissez-faire attitude can have disastrous consequences, leading us to ignore the signposts and waymarks that can guide towards better chances, enrichment and fulfilment.

KEEPING A JOURNAL

One of the most illuminating ways of reflecting on our lives is to keep a journal, or 'journaling', as it is often known. This is different from keeping a diary, which merely notes down the outward facts and events. In journaling you keep a record of your thoughts and responses to your experiences and circumstances, which provide useful material for reflection. Your journal tracks the pathway, if you like, of your developing self. Then, later during times of quiet and retreat (metaphorical lay-bys), your journal provides a vital tool for evaluating your life, acting as a kind of map so that you can trace and evaluate your past and pinpoint emerging directional markers.

If you already keep a diary detailing your day-to-day activity, it might simply be a matter of adding personal reflections to this. There are, however, good-quality journals and notebooks available that provide a bigger space for you not just to write but to scribble, draw, and stick in images and cuttings as well – almost like a scrapbook.

Figure 9.1 Your journal can be not only a key ingredient in your times of solitude, but also a vital tool in your journey towards inner peace.

Try it now: Start a journal

If you are not used to recording thoughts and reflections, it can be a little daunting at first sitting before all those blank pages wondering what and how to write. In part, it's just a question of getting into the habit, so start small and simply at first. So:

✳ Find yourself a small, but beautifully formed, notebook.

✳ Carry it with you, in your briefcase or handbag.

✳ Write the day's date.

✳ During random quiet moments take your journal out and record things you see, hear and experience as well as the feelings and thoughts these experiences stir in you. It's not always necessary to use words – try drawing something that represents your thoughts and feelings instead.

✳ Note down the good things that are to come that day, or that have already happened to you.

✳ Think about your hopes, desires, fears or concerns for the coming days and weeks etc.

✳ During longer periods of quiet – during a retreat perhaps or down in that garden shed – reread your journal and begin to piece together your 'story' and look out for the signposts (see below).

Quantity is not something to aim for – you will find this comes as you limber up and get used to representing your thoughts in written or visual form. Gradually, brain and hand co-ordinate in a free-flowing way (something I find is rather inhibited by keyboard-based thinking and writing), enabling you to write and think more fluidly. Eventually, keeping your journal will become a fluid psychomotor action of mind feeding hand, hand feeding mind.

Don't make keeping a journal a forced thing. Just do it during quiet moments, on the bus, waiting at the dentist, or during short quiet moments at the beginning or the end of the day. You will surprise yourself just how quickly your writing begins to develop and you begin to see patterns within your thinking and experiences.

Later, when you have accrued many days, months or even years of commentary and reflection, you will come to see your life story unfold, in your own words, before you. You will see the fears that came to nothing, challenges that provoked action or change, joyous occasions that filled you with delight and gratitude, and the times of sadness and loss... all will be there. You will have a map of your life and the signposts and waymarks will be clearly visible.

Maps and waymarks

Today many of us have lost the art of reading a map, relying instead on satellite navigation systems to show us the way from A to B. We ignore the plain signs in front of our eyes and listen instead to a monotonous disembodied voice issuing instructions. What better metaphor for the unreflecting and disengaged attitude with which we travel through life today, where the journey is all about the destination and not the quality of the travelling itself?

Our journals can help us reconnect with our lives, providing us maps over which we can pore, and in which we discover new landscapes and work out alternative routes and paths.

Remember this: Ditch the satnav

A metaphorical satellite navigation system is not always the best option as we journey through life. We can use peacefulness to become alert to the signals and signposts that point towards a more fulfilling life.

Let's pursue our journal/map correlation a bit further. During a retreat or other period of solitude, look at your 'map' and ask yourself the following:

▶ What is my destination?

▶ In which direction will I be going?

▶ What does each stage of the journey teach me?

▶ Am I making sufficient stops to gain a better perspective on my journey?

There are times in life when this kind of reflection comes about naturally – a time of ill-health or change in circumstances for example. Times of change or transition, such as the move from childhood to adulthood, from employment to retirement, from singledom to marriage, and back again, along with a myriad of others, create natural waymarks. These form clear stage-of-life junctions at which we can make decisions about which direction we are going to head in – left, right, ahead or even back again. Other waymarks are less obvious, however, and we need to keep our eyes peeled. If we don't take regular opportunities to take a look at the whole map, you can be blissfully unaware of the route you may somewhat inadvertently have taken.

Try it now: Look an old photograph of yourself

Change is a constant in our lives, and we should be prepared for it to come into view. If you take a look at an older photograph of yourself, taken three years, 13 years or 30 years ago, what do you see? There is change before your eyes. Change you have not noticed in your day-to-day journeying along.

Occasionally, when my present husband and I go walking and I say I want to stop to admire the view, he will tease me, telling me that I really only want to catch my breath. There may be some truth in this, especially as I get older, but nonetheless I would argue that stopping to recover after a long steep climb is no bad thing anyway. We do not *have* to be constantly hurrying to our destination, and taking in the view can be useful as well as pleasurable. You can take stock of your progress, assess the lay of the land and confirm your direction of travel.

Signposts for peacefulness

As on any long journey, a comfort break or two is necessary. You need to stretch the legs, and nourish and refresh the body. Similarly, such times must not be taken lightly in your life journey, if peacefulness is to be attained. After all, corners cut or missed are dangerous. During such times you are able to recognize and respect the many and varied signposts that lead towards the peaceful life. Let's look at some of these now.

SIGNPOST 1: SLEEP

Sleep is something that frequently gets eroded as we try to squeeze in all the activities we want, or feel duty-bound, to take part in in our busy lives. It is easy to stay up just a little later to watch a film, socialize with friends, get through a piece of work. Even if you see these activities as something you *have* to do, they are in fact occupations which emanate from the culmination of many previous choices made about how you want to work, and how you choose to socialize and occupy yourself, particularly in terms of responsibilities to family, friends and leisure pursuits.

Try, instead, to treat sleep with the respect it deserves; don't try to cut corners and burn the candle at both ends. Sleep is a necessary part of an active, successful life, and is not simply about rest. With advances in brain imaging and monitoring, we now understand much more about the amazing behaviour of the brain during sleep and the chemical processes that take place:

During sleep the brain releases new combinations of the hormones and chemical messengers that stimulate cellular activity throughout the body. At some times the sleeping brain actually appears to be more active than it is while awake, burning large quantities of sugar and oxygen as neurons fire rapidly.

William C. Dement, *The Promise of Sleep: The scientific connection between health, happiness and a good night's sleep*

SIGNPOST 2: FEEDING MIND AND BODY

The body, mind and soul are fed through doing, being and belonging, as well as by food. So, the things you choose to learn, read, do and explore, particularly with regard to quality and quantity, will provide nourishment for the soul. As an individual, it is important to choose the things that best suit your interests, yes, but which also challenge and stretch the boundaries in ways that encourage you to learn and grow. Respect for the natural world is a particular soul feeder – spend time in it and it will restore you.

SIGNPOST 3: VARIETY ADDS SPICE

Changes in pace, time and variety of activity through the course of a day, week, month are refreshing, energizing, satisfying and motivating. If you spend long periods of time at the same or similar tasks or occupations, your body and mind will eventually suffer. Variety brings a spice to life. This does not mean overfilling your life with a surfeit of variety but offering it a balance of different 'ingredients'.

SIGNPOST 4: MAKING CHOICES

Just as a houseplant needs certain conditions to thrive and grow, even in the sheltered environment of a room, so do we need a balance of conditions to be fully nourished for success. The plant, of course, has no choice over its environment. It cannot de-select; it relies on what we give it and has no free will to choose. Unlike plants, we humans can make choices. The risk, however, is that such choices can frequently be dictated by whimsical or fanciful notions, or ideals imposed upon is by societal and commercial forces, rather than actual biological needs.

Solitude and peacefulness brings us back to a point of greater discernment, away from distractions and back to our natural basic needs – for space, time, food, water, warmth...

SIGNPOST 5: PEACEFUL PLEASURES

Simple pleasures have the effect of automatically slowing us down, leading us to peacefulness. These are not of the quick-fix kind that burn out as quickly as they arrive, like the gratification we get when we buy a new pair of shoes, but of the longer-lasting and lingering kind which usually engages us both sensually and spiritually. It may be walking by the coastline, dipping your toes in the crystal-clear waters of a stream, feeling the warmth and acceptance of a pet as you stroke its fur, or listening to a haunting tune. Those small and simple pleasures, which strike a chord in your heart and soul, are signposts that beckon you towards peacefulness. Make sure there is space and time in your days, every day, for at least one such pleasure.

SIGNPOST 6: RITUALS

Introducing, or reintroducing, rituals into our everyday lives creates a rhythm that nourishes and inspires. Rituals help to slow us down, sharpening our sensual engagement with the present and reconnecting us with our past by evoking memories. Ritual expands our experience of time.

Take, for example, the everyday task of making a hot drink of tea or coffee. Do you usually reach for a jar of 'instant' or a teabag, pour on the hot water, and, hey presto, you have an instant cuppa? By turning making a hot drink into a ritual over which we take time and care, we can deepen our experience of the everyday and of time itself. Try the following:

▶ *Make real tea* – engage with the process of choosing the right kind of tea, preparing it, smelling it, brewing it, and then pouring it into a pre-warmed teacup. Carried out with attention and care, it makes sitting back and enjoying the tea all the more pleasurable.

▶ *Make real coffee* – rather than an instant.

▶ *Make real bread* – rather than eating the shop-bought variety.

▶ *Rear your own plants* – rather than getting them from a nursery or garden centre.

There are hundreds of other ways of gaining simple pleasure from being more deeply involved and connected with everyday activities. This will have a profound effect on you cognitively and draw you towards peacefulness.

SIGNPOST 7: ROUTINE

Routine facilitates peacefulness through structure and anticipation. Routine is like a rhythm or sequence in our everyday life. Babies and children are particularly comfortable with routine. As human beings we are predisposed to respond positively to rhythm and rhythmic sounds or actions – heart beats, a ticking clock, the gentle sway of a boat, the ebb and flow of the tide on a beach, music; all these have the power to give us a deep, age-old sense of security, as when we were gently cradled in our mother's womb. By introducing more routine to everyday life, you are more likely to reduce stress and pressure and find yourself in tune with nature.

Try it now: List *your* signposts

The seven signposts above, I believe, are important factors in any journey towards peacefulness, but they are of course in some sense *mine. Your* signposts may share similarities with mine but there may be a difference in emphasis and some may not play any role for you at all. Make a list of the signposts that help to steer *you* to peacefulness. Place it on your desk, pin board, or in your organizer, as a reminder. Here is a checklist to help you:

✽ having an open mind
✽ periods of solitude
✽ making a retreat
✽ a simple, quiet space
✽ keeping a journal
✽ using reflective and/or relaxation exercises
✽ enjoying simple pleasures
✽ adding more rituals to everyday life
✽ keeping to routines
✽ immersing myself in the natural world
✽ having a hobby
✽ engaging in meaningful work.

Focus points

* Your story is unique and can teach you peacefulness.
* Take time to pause and take in the 'view' of your life.
* Find the signposts that can guide you towards peacefulness.
* Routines and rituals can enrich and deepen your experience of the everyday, filling it with both memory and anticipation.

Next step

You may have some questions at this point, such as:

* How can I prevent my self from side-lining times of solitude?
* What will keep me on a peaceful track?
* Will I be able to notice changes in me?

The pathway to peacefulness is not always smooth. As you note and record your story, mapping out the responses and discoveries you make along the way, you will probably notice that there are things that repeatedly threaten to sabotage your solitude and peacefulness. We will look at some of these in the next, and final, chapter...

10

Preventing Solitude Sabotage

In this chapter you will learn:

▶ *about what prevents our progress towards solitude and peacefulness*

▶ *about taming guilt, desire and temptation.*

How do you feel?

Before you begin this chapter, ask yourself the following questions:

1 How do you separate your busyness and solitude times?

2 What often hijacks your alone time?

3 What tempts you away from solitude?

4 Do you feel guilty about taking time to yourself?

5 How do you safeguard your alone time?

When supposedly enjoying their hard-earned leisure, people generally report surprisingly low moods; yet they keep on wishing for more leisure.

Mihaly Csikszentmihalyi, *Flow: the classic work on how to achieve happiness*

As the above quote suggests, even though we desire something – for example, the desire to be alone now and again – when we finally do get it, we sometimes find that our expectations have not been fulfilled and our desire returns unabated. It is therefore important for us to work out exactly what threatens to sabotage our experience of solitude and thus ensure that its real benefits are felt and enjoyed.

What prevents progress towards solitude and peacefulness?

Other than the obvious answers such as work and family commitments, there are other less obvious things, generally of our own making, that sabotage our path towards peacefulness. I like to call these factors 'bandits', which waylay us and rob us of chances of finding peacefulness. Lack of mental and physical preparedness, not prioritizing time for solitude, or simply not properly appreciating its benefits are also among the most common 'bandits'. Let's look at some of these now.

Remember this: Watch out for bandits!

Be prepared for the bandits that lie in wait as you attempt your journey towards peacefulness.

FAILURE TO SET ASIDE TIME

Unless you regularly schedule in periods of solitude into your life, you are unlikely ever to get round to creating them. Creating the conditions for solitude takes time and thoughtful preparation – simply trusting in happenstance to hand you solitude on a plate will not work.

Commit time for solitude in your schedule. Write it in your diary. Tell others your plans.

FAILURE TO PREPARE FOR TRANSITION

When I introduce people to the notion of quiet days or periods I often suggest using symbolic everyday items to signify that we are moving towards peacefulness. For example, taking off your wristwatch and placing it in a basket out of the way can be a ritual that signifies a change in priority. Actions like this form a transitional gateway between our busy everyday lives and silent solitary time.

I once watched a professional storyteller who signalled the beginning of his storytelling time by laying down a rug and taking off his shoes. This signified that he and his listeners were about to enter a different world where different rules came into play. We as listeners were being invited to tune in and to truly listen for the space of an hour or so. In a similar way, you will need to create markers for yourself that signify the beginning and end of solitary time, especially when you are taking only a half-hour or an hour out.

Try creating a gateway to solitude by:

▶ taking the phone off the hook or switching off your mobile

▶ taking off your watch

▶ lighting a candle

- preparing a comfortable space
- closing the door of the room
- taking a slow walk beforehand, either around the garden or around a short circuit near your home or office.

FAILURE TO PREPARE PSYCHOLOGICALLY

Psychological preparation is vital; we cannot simply expect to cast off our everyday frame of mind in a moment. The following exercise should help arm you against this particular bandit.

Try it now: Cast off distractions

✳ Write down any frustrations and things that may be absorbing or rattling you on a piece of paper as one-word titles. Fold the paper up and place it in a box out of sight.

✳ Relax with some soft music first, to slow yourself down and sooth your mind.

✳ Become mindful of silence, and allow troubling thoughts to disappear; this is where a lit candle, picture or sculpture as a focus of contemplation can help.

✳ Allay your fears of being alone by reminding yourself of the practical benefits. Ask yourself:

▷ What do I want from quietness and solitude?

▷ What works for me? What doesn't?

▷ What do I want to change?

▷ What decisive action can I take right now to make the experience work better for me?

FAILURE TO FIND THE RIGHT SPACE

Place and space can disrupt our feelings of peacefulness. When we are alone, this is even more noticeable. Places or spaces that are messy, overfilled, out of balance or incongruent do not instil calm. Calm and pleasant surroundings allow the mind to feel more content and satisfied – we relax because the mind feels surrounded by simplicity and tranquillity.

Case study

I was taking some time out in a small chapel at the back of my city's cathedral when a young man of about 16 years came and sat opposite me. He was, he told me, planning a website he was launching and had come to the cathedral to find inspiration. He told me that he was not religious. Having attended the cathedral school for many years, he'd been 'forced' (his word) to come to the place every day for prayers. But now, rather than hating the space, he found it somewhere he could be himself and not be distracted by outside concerns. This place had become a place of inspiration for him. Sitting before a huge modern stained-glass window, he was touched creatively. He could draw from the environment and tune into his own being, 'far from the madding crowd'.

FAILURE TO SET ASIDE OTHERS' NEEDS

We destroy our inner peace when we allow others' goals and strivings to ensnare us – by association we are caught up in the web of *their* busyness, taking on desires, strivings or goals that are not our own. For example, this can happen within groups of friends, in clubs, societies, organizations and businesses as well as within our circle of family and friends. Our personal time is absorbed by others' expectations.

Others' needs and strivings will gradually take over our life if we let them and that is not what a life well lived should be. Be prepared to collaborate and co-operate, certainly, but do not allow others to control or manipulate your time and tasks.

FAILURE TO SET BOUNDARIES

Unfortunately, modern living encourages us to have 'butterfly minds'. Some of us are almost forced into being a butterfly because of the sheer range and quantity of tasks we expect or are expected to do in a day. Time-saving gadgets and gizmos give us the opportunity to flit hither and thither rather like an insect gathering nectar. We hop from plant to plant and are rarely still for more than a second. All this can sabotage our inner peacefulness.

Clarity and clear distinctions between different activities are not only important for the successful achievement of tasks, but also help to protect against distraction and the stress of confusion. Making clean breaks between tasks and different types of activity aids peacefulness of mind.

Temptation, guilt and the myth of success

Inadequate preparation, butterfly-like behaviour and so on can easily scupper our chances of finding peacefulness, but altogether more destructive are the powerful forces that shape modern life. These truly are the big-time bandits that prey on peacefulness and, unless we get them under control, we have little chance of achieving our goal.

TEMPTATION

In today's world temptation abounds. A shiny new car, a fashionable dress, the stylish watch – such things are hard to resist when they are constantly dangled before our eyes. I freely admit that I have personally desired nice cars – their graceful elegance, the possibility of speed, the status they bestow; it is perfectly normal to appreciate and be attracted to beautiful things and the way they make you feel. However, when such desires begin to overwhelm you and become the be-all and end-all, then your chances of finding satisfaction, contentment and inner peace are well and truly sabotaged.

Times of solitude can help you reflect on what is really of lasting importance and value in your life, enabling you to affirm those relationships and experiences that are rich with value. Peacefulness teaches you that you can obtain a different, non-monetary kind of wealth by leading you away from temptation into a gracefulness of living that feeds contentment, not resentment.

Typically, marketing and advertising play not just on our desires but on our guilt as well. For example, Father's Day, Mother's Day, Valentine's Day and Christmas are all classic times of the year when our guilt is pricked by the product promoters. We buy out of guilt – if we know we are busy and neglecting someone a little, we redress the balance and assuage the guilt by buying a present.

Don't fall for the guilt trip. Don't think I *must* buy a card, a present, a treat, etc. What really matters is having a clear mind that causes you to behave the way *you* choose, not the way the marketers want you to. Of course, there are important and significant events and people in our lives, and it is important to acknowledge our gratitude and joy for them, but this does not necessarily require or demand indulgence.

Remember this: Watch out for guilt trips

In silence and solitude reflect on and see beyond guilt-inducing subliminal messages.

THE MYTH OF SUCCESS

Success is not just the balance in your bank, or the stripes on your arm, or your position on the corporate ladder, but the ability to craft, endure and enjoy life. Wholeness, sincerity and integrity are the factors that lead to real and lasting successes in life, not how many exams you've passed. If it is forced, through hot-housing, pushing others aside, or ingratiating yourself, success may only be temporary before eventually loneliness, isolation and perhaps depression creep in, sabotaging our chances of finding inner peace.

Try it now: Evaluate a success

Try evaluating an action you've taken today. Look at whether you achieved what you set out to do. Identify the deeper motivation behind it.

In his illuminating book *They F*** You Up* (Bloomsbury 2002), the clinical psychologist Oliver James relates adversity in early childhood to a 'fanatical commitment to success'; in particular, those with a 'weak sense of self, resulting from unempathic care in infancy' are liable to traits such as impatience, novelty-seeking, compulsiveness and controlling behaviours. The drive to succeed, in terms of power or wealth particularly, may therefore be motivated by deeply negative feelings and motivations.

No wonder peacefulness does not feature prominently in our success-driven culture. If a childhood has lacked love and attachment, the adult will be focused solely and obsessively on outward achievement, eventually leading him or her to be filled by an aching need for something more. It is no surprise to witness many successful or high-achieving individuals frequently searching for spiritual and therapeutic solutions to fill the void of their empty, hollow experiences and feelings. Perhaps the practice of solitude can provide something for them, too.

Case study

A lady who came to me for coaching was working as a senior manager in a large organization. She had been increasingly feeling that her work was no longer fulfilling her. She'd not achieved particularly highly at school and studied throughout her adult life, after she'd had her family, to compensate. Now studying for a Master's she still did not feel that this was enough, though further qualifications were not necessary to her career. It was as if she could not get off the treadmill of having to prove to herself that she was able to achieve. Career success had not fulfilled her inner longing.

Try it now: Safeguarding peacefulness

Use the following quick checklist to help safeguard your peacefulness:

* Seek perspective in all situations.
* Avoid micro-measuring time.
* Clean out emotionally driven responses such as fear, anxiety, guilt and shame.
* Feel gratitude and pride for where you are *now*.
* Graciously accept your circumstances as a part of life and the place from where to embark on different pathways.
* Find contentment in the simpler things of life such as walking or just sitting still in a quiet place.
* The natural world will teach you much – connect with it!
* Think: 'Nothing and no one is going to sabotage my peacefulness!'

Souvenirs of solitude

To close this book, I want to share one final technique with you that I have found to be particularly invaluable as I have striven to carry the benefits of my time in solitude back into the busyness of my daily life. During your times of solitude or retreat, it will often happen that you will come across an object that catches your attention – a shell on a beach, for example, or a particular view – or something that enables you to hone in on your inner peace – a poem, for example, or a beautiful bowl. Collect or make a record of these things – put the shell in your pocket, draw or photograph the view, copy out the poem on a special piece of paper, and so on.

These are the 'souvenirs of solitude' that you will be able to take home with you. These souvenirs are not like the 'cheap and cheerful' knick-knacks we sometimes bring back from our holidays, but something altogether more enduring and meaningful. Collect them together in a beautiful box, perhaps one you have decorated yourself. During quiet moments – at the end of the day, for example – open your box and explore!

Figure 10.1 Souvenirs of solitude: Peaceful times can be recaptured through meditation, using a box of special objects collected during retreats.

You will find that your 'souvenirs', if carefully and thoughtfully chosen, have the power to reawaken and recharge the feelings of peacefulness and oneness that you discovered in retreat.

Treasure these things! They are deeply *yours*. What is right for you is yours to hold and enjoy – let no man or woman let you feel regretful of it.

Focus points

✳ Set the scene for time out by organizing your time and thoughts.

✳ Guilt, desire and temptation all steal peacefulness.

✳ Check the motivation that lies behind your desire for success.

✳ Don't let the peacefulness bandits sabotage your journey.

Next step

You should now be ready to experiment with times of solitude and to find your own path towards peacefulness. To help you, at the end of this book you will find some additional exercises (Appendix 2) as well as extra resources in the form of suggestions for further reading and recommended websites.

Good luck on your journey!

Resources

Listed here is a small selection of further resources – both books and websites – to enable you to develop awareness, peacefulness and a mindful approach to living.

Reading

Bach, R., *The Bridge across Forever* (Pan Macmillan 1984)

Carr, N., 'Rural > City > Cyberspace: The Biggest Migration In Human History', available online at www.adbusters.org/magazine/99/nicholas-carr-migration-human.html

Claxton, G., *Hare Brain Tortoise Mind* (London 1998)

Csikszentmihalyi, M., *Flow: The classic work on how to achieve happiness* (Random House 2002)

Coperthwaite, W.S., *A Handmade Life* (Chelsea Green Publishing 2007)

Donaldson, M., *Children's Minds* (Fontana Press 1988)

Exley, H., *...And Wisdom Comes Quietly* (Exley 2000)

Gladwell, M., *Blink: The Power of Thinking Without Thinking* (Penguin 2005)

James, O., *They F*** You Up* (Bloomsbury 2002)

Jamison, Abbot, C., *Finding Happiness: Monastic steps for a fulfilling life* (Phoenix 2009)

Kennerley, H., *Overcoming Anxiety: A self-help guide using cognitive behavioural techniques* (Robinson 1997)

Large, M., *Who's Bringing Them Up?: How to break the TV habit* (Hawthorn Press 1990)

Maitland, S., *A Book of Silence* (Granta 2009)

Merton, T., *No Man Is an Island* (Harcourt 1982)

Moore, T., *A Life at Work: The joy of discovering what you were born to do* (Piatkus 2008)

Neuberg, A. and Waldman, M.R., *How God Changes Your Brain* (Balantine Books 2010)

Ogilvy, J., *Turning Points: Stories to change your life* (Lion Hudson 2010)

Lane, J., *The Spirit of Silence: Making space for creativity* (Green Books 2011)

Loehr, J. and Schwartz, T., *The Power of Full Engagement* (Simon and Schuster 2005)

Ozaniec, N., *Beat Stress with Meditation*, Teach Yourself (Hodder & Stoughton 2010)

Parke, S., *Recovering the Power of Alone* (White Crow Books 2011)

Peck, M.S., *The Road Less Travelled* (Random House 1990)

Pink, D.H., *A Whole New Mind* (Marshall Cavendish 2010)

Rolheiser, R., *Seeking Spirtuality* (Hodder and Stoughton 1998)

Storr, A., *Solitude* (Flamingo 1988)

Syed, M., Bounce: *The Myth of Talent and the Power of Practice* (Fourth Estate 2011)

Tom, D., *Find the Balance: Essential steps to fulfilment in your work and life* (BBC 2004)

de Waal, E., *Seeking God* (Collins 2007)

Warren, J., *Headtrip* (Oneworld 2007)

Wilding, C. and Milne, A., *Cognitive Behavioural Therapy*, Teach Yourself (Hodder & Stoughton 2010)

Williams, M. and Penman, D., *Mindfulness: A guide to finding peace in a frantic world* (Piatkus 2011)

Websites

GENERAL

www.goodreads.com – insightful book recommendations and comment. Helps you locate books within the genre you're interested in.

www.livinglifefully.com – provides a collection of online resources containing wisdom from those who have gone before. Poetry, quotations and reflections help you discover a fuller life through beauty and wonder.

RETREATS

www.thegoodretreatguide.com – an online guide to taking a retreat at various locations across Europe and beyond. Also includes information about different spiritual practices and meditation techniques.

www.lovelifenow.com – offers retreat weekends during which you can learn the art of mindfulness.

www.quietgarden.org – offers an international network of local garden spaces available for personal silence, reflection and prayer.

COACHING

www.parallaxuk.com – executive and leadership coaching to enhance resilience and decision-making and build creative capability at work.

www.goodlifecoaching.com – experienced coach Sharon Good offers supportive life coaching and classes in a range of areas, including career change, writing and creativity.

Appendix 1:
A 'menu' of retreats

The following menu of options and suggestions for short
and longer 'self-coaching' solitary retreats should help you
to find one that is right for you. Choose from short or longer
stop times. If you are not used to taking solitary retreats, it
is advisable to start with short periods first. Whatever the
length, however, all of these solitary times should be treated
as sacrosanct and you should allow nothing and no one to
interfere with them or take precedence over them.

A coffee stop

This takes no longer than the time it takes for a cuppa. Each
morning for one week, before you do anything else, spend
15 minutes sitting still, alone, by a window, a view, or outside.
Set your alarm clock 15 minutes earlier if necessary, but make
sure you do nothing but sit quietly without anyone else around.
As thoughts or worries come into your mind, intercept them
and let them go (this gets easier over time). It might help to
repeat a single word to yourself such as 'peace' or 'calm'. After
one week, try the exercise again, but this time have a book of
beautiful images open in front of you or a poem to read and
contemplate. This is the perfect way to relax before you start
the day.

You could also do these 15-minute coffee stop retreats during
the day. The idea is to become mindful of the moment and
enjoy preparing yourself serenely for work and engagement.

A lunchtime linger

This is a one-hour stop that requires a little more preparation.
Prioritize in your diary a one-hour break, at either lunchtime
or another suitable part of the day. It is important to schedule

the time in, otherwise it will be jettisoned for other activity. If necessary, tell a family member, a friend or a colleague what you plan to do so that it makes you more likely to do it. Choose a peaceful place in the home or office, or close by, or even drive to a place with a view (a seafront or beauty spot). Have ready a few items – soft music, your journal and a pen. Sit awhile, or walk and become aware of all the things around you. Think about how these things, whether plants and trees or objects in the home, give you pleasure and how you relate to them. Reflect on your silence and the inspiration the environment gives you. In your journal write down any thoughts, or sketch out any images, that this time gives you.

The idea here is to raise your sensory awareness and appreciation and get you more used to peaceful solitude.

A half-day of quietness

It is well worth while to take yourself away for longer retreat times. Away from your usual surroundings you are more receptive and less tempted to catch up on that much neglected job around the house. There are places that allow you to visit just for a half- or whole day. Some are led by faith-based organizations but are open to all. Or you can just take a trip to the countryside or an inspiring building. It may be to a place that holds special meaning for you such as a cathedral, a familiar place by the sea or in a park. Tell friends, colleagues or family what you are proposing to do and schedule it into the diary. Take with you painting or drawing materials if you feel so inclined, as well as a bottle of water or soft drink. Essential is your journal in which you can write down your thoughts and ideas, or simply doodle. Engage with the environment you choose to go to, but do not engage in any activity other than solitary walking, sitting and (if by the sea) paddling your toes.

The idea is to engage with the rhythm of the environment, the flow of a river, the turn of a tide, the passage of people, but not to be an involved part of it. Relax and enjoy a walk or some quiet painting or writing time. Soak up the atmosphere.

The one-day wander

This is much like the half-day described above. Again drive to a meaningful place – perhaps it may be a little further away, somewhere you played as a young child or a place you have had a holiday, somewhere with happy memories. Again, prepare beforehand by informing friends and relatives, and take along your journal and other creative materials as well as a picnic of simple food and soft drink. Walk/stroll/sit/picnic – engage in the rhythm of doing these things within the environment, mindfully and openly. Read an inspiring book. Remember to ignore your mobile phone. You have told others that you will be in solitude today so they should respect your wish not to be contacted. The idea is to get used to being by yourself, even if there are people nearby. You are alone, standing apart from others though they are near. Record your thoughts and feelings of peacefulness as you respond to the environment and the memories and associations it conjures up for you.

A simple week

Plan a five-day retreat during the working week. Again, telling friends, family and colleagues will not only keep you accountable for doing it but will also help them to respect your need for no communication during this time. Make sure you treat this long retreat as special and important – a sanctuary time. Book a five-day break in a small cottage or caravan where you can be alone. This does not have to be a long way from home – a 20-minute journey time is fine, just as long as you can be totally alone. If you feel vulnerable, do this with one other person at first, before taking the leap alone. The most important thing is to reduce activity, connectivity and distractions. So, take only food that is fresh and does not need cooking. Travel light with just a few books, your journal, a relaxation CD and gentle music, a candle to help with contemplation. Take only simple, comfy clothes. Try to reduce everything down to a minimum. At first you may find such minimalist packing a challenge but keep in mind that your goal is to live as simply as possible for five days. Spend your days reading, going for short walks, preparing food and eating mindfully, resting, writing and reflecting. The idea is for you to begin to notice that without the clutter and with a simple lifestyle, you become more inspired. Do not put on any gadgets or technology that connects you to the outside world. The idea is to clear your thoughts and mind of the clutter of news and entertainment, and to be inspired and motivated by the experience instead.

Appendix 2:
Self-reflective exercises

It is sometimes useful to focus on more structured self-reflective exercises, particularly if you are not used to being alone for longer periods of time. They can help to focus the mind in specific ways if you want to be a little more directed during your quiet time. They can also be used as simple self-diagnostic tests, helping you to find out about what motivates you, what your priorities are and how your lifestyle may, or may not, be contributing to peacefulness.

Here and now

Answer the following questions and record the answers in your journal:

▶ What are the most significant things happening to you now (both good and not so good)?

▶ How would you like things to be different? By when?

▶ What is preventing you from achieving this?

▶ What are your fears/insecurities about making any changes you need to make?

▶ Name three things over which you procrastinate that could help you make those changes?

▶ What are your available resources, in terms of both your talents and more practical things, that will help you achieve your goal?

Awareness walk

Take a 15-minute walk in the garden or an open space. Preferably remove your shoes and stockings. Feel the grass or hard surface beneath your feet. Recognize the awakening of your responses to your surroundings, the natural world around you. Tune in to what you see, hear, smell and feel. Breathe in deeply. Walk slowly and purposefully. Notice things around you, but do not get caught into thinking about them, just let your thoughts focus on the movement of your body and its contact with the earth. As you come to the end of your walk, stop. Stand still and simply raise your arms above your head in a stretch, and breathe in and out once, deeply. As you do so, imagine you are breathing in all the energy and freshness of the natural world about you and then exhale any internal stresses and strains.

You may choose to journal your responses to this exercise. Record what was important physically, emotionally, cognitively and spiritually, as you awoke to your environment.

Life balance

Think about the areas of life where your energy is focused. Copy out and fill in the grid below. First write down percentages to represent how much of your energy is taken up by each area. Then record the percentage of peacefulness this involvement gives you followed by the percentage by which you would like to raise the amount of peacefulness. Finally, write down a comment about what you could do now to increase peacefulness in each area in order of priority.

	Work	Home	Social	Friends	Family
% of energy					
% of peacefulness					
% to raise					
Comment					

Index